EMPOWERED FAITH

~~~❦~~~

How to Sow God's Love and Truth in Everyday Life

SALLY KEIRAN

Empowered Faith

© 2025 by Sally Keiran

All Rights Reserved

MASTER
P R E S S

Unless otherwise indicated, Scripture quotations are from:

The Holy Bible, New International Version (NIV)

© 1973, 1984, by International Bible Society,

used by permission of Zondervan Publishing House

Printed in the United States

ISBN 978-0-9993750-8-2

For information:

MASTER PRESS

3405 ISLAND BAY WAY, KNOXVILLE, TN 37931

Mail to: publishing@masterpressbooks.com

Endorsements

In *Empowered Faith*, Sally paints a beautiful and encouraging picture of the goodness of God and the opportunities He gives us to share His divine love. This book shows just how many places God allows us to experience Him and use His people to share His message in everyday life. You will get goosebumps, laugh, and shed tears as you witness "Jehovah Sneaky" in the pages of this book. I highly recommend anyone wanting to know how to share God 's love in their everyday life to read this book.

Greg Ealey, Th.M
Campus Pastor, Colonial Presbyterian Church, Kansas City, Missouri

Would you like to know how God works through willing people? Would you like to see God work through you? If yes, this book is for you. Filled with examples of God using an ordinary woman to do the extraordinary, Sally challenges her readers to make the most of every opportunity.

Rear Admiral Barry C. Black
Chaplain of the United States Senate

Empowered Faith will provide insight from a fearless Ambassador who is a role model of what it means to be all-in for the gospel and on mission everywhere you go

G. Moroney
Author of *Living in His Presence*

In *Empowered Faith*, Sally Keiran beautifully illustrates how Jesus can bring light to the darkest corners of our lives, weaving threads of beauty and purpose through our brokenness. As she shares touching vignettes from her years of ministry and family life, Sally takes readers on a journey of hope, revealing the extraordinary ways in which redemption and grace can flourish amidst our deepest struggles.

Lee McMahon
Consultant for Evangelization, Archdiocese of Kansas City

Through parables and narratives, Jesus unveiled deep truths. Similarly, in *Empowered Faith* Sally Keiran shares miraculous encounters where the Holy Spirit's power vividly manifests. Her stories of divine appointments, where she served as an instrument of God's love, will embolden, encourage, and inspire you. This book is not merely a collection of experiences; it's a bright beacon of hope and a testament to God's ceaseless intervention in our times of need.

We reside in a world desperately yearning for God's touch, "for such a time as this" (Esther 4:14). Sally Keiran is a beacon of God's light, and this book offers an easy to read yet profound message that places you at the corner of Hope and How-To. Immerse yourself in these pages, and then step out and sow seeds of God's love and truth in everyday life.

Dan Snell
Author of The Winsome Way, The Winsome Candidate, Speaker,
Broadcaster

Sally Keiran's creativity and boldness in sharing the Good News of our redemption in Jesus Christ is an inspiration to all believers.

Kurt Pfotenhauer
Board Member, LifeSong Christian Fellowship

Welcome to witnessing for Christ as a divinely appointed and Spirit empowered adventure! This is what Sally offers us in her new book loaded with vivid personal accounts which will amaze, amuse, instruct, and inspire. You will meet a broad cross section of people and circumstances where the Lord opened doors and hearts to the power of the gospel message through Sally's courage and willingness to engage. The Lord provided her with some tools that may surprise you as they did her. I think this book will change the way God's people touch the world for Christ!

Polly Barlow
Prayer Leader, Moms in Prayer International, Burke, Virginia

A page turner, *Empowered Faith* is chock-full of real-life stories that empower readers to share God's love and truth in everyday life as conduits of His life force, channels of His grace, and reflections of His presence. Narratives illustrate how readers may prayerfully appropriate the supernatural power of the Holy Spirit to live in divine synchronicity with God—looking for Him in the details of their lives, listening to His voice, and acting on His promptings. Shared anecdotes remind readers who and whose they are in Christ and their purpose as ambassadors from Heaven to Earth, soldiers in His Salvation Army, and mere sojourners in this world.

Richard E. Beyer, PhD
Founder and Managing Member, INTEGRITAS®

Looking for some motivation to step out in faith and start spiritual conversations with people? *Empowered Faith* can offer plenty! The stories and encounters that Sally tells in *Empowered Faith* show how the Lord used her time and time again to share the gospel with people in everyday life. God is already at work in people's lives, and He wants to use ordinary people like us to reach them.

Scott & Patti Neel
CRU - Church Movements

Contents

Acknowledgments

With deep gratitude to my loving Heavenly Father who gave me the privilege to be married to one of the great seed sowers in the Kingdom of God. Alan Keiran loved to make Christ known, sowing seeds of kindness, hope, and truth everywhere he went. Whether walking amidst the troops in Kuwait during Desert Storm, serving on Capitol Hill, or riding on the DC Metro train, he reflected Christ faithfully. He was a bold, radiant witness throughout his life, serving twenty-three years as a Navy chaplain and nine years as Chief of Staff for the U.S. Senate Chaplain Barry Black before Alan's eternal homegoing in December 2020.

A special thanks to my dear friend Abigail Knutson, who was my editor for this book as well as my first book, *Out of Suffering into Glory.* You were such a blessing to me with your encouragement and helpful suggestions as we progressed chapter to chapter. It was a joy to work together on this project, and I am so grateful for your help and friendship. Thank you, my friend!

Much thanks to my daughter Jennifer and son John and their families for their support, love, and encouragement. Thanks for all the prayers and walking together in losing Dad—our inspiration for living the authentic Christian life.

Thanks also to my dear sister Irene and my wonderful friends all over the country who have prayed for me and Alan throughout our years of ministry and now lift up prayers for me as I continue to walk in faith, follow the Holy Spirit, and seek to make Christ known wherever I go.

Thank you, my dear Lord Jesus, for the privilege to be Your witness during my days on earth. How grateful I am that You rescued me from sin, hopelessness, and from the darkness of my soul and brought me into Your glorious Kingdom of Light. Thank You, Holy Spirit for Your indwelling, Your supernatural power, gifts and anointing. And thank You Father, for loving me, for strengthening me, and for Your abiding presence. All glory, honor and praise to You!

Foreword

Do you remember the old saying WWJD ("What Would Jesus Do?") Well, WWSD ("What Would Sally Do?") is my version. I am not an extrovert by nature. Sure, I love to talk a lot to my closest friends, but when I meet a stranger, I get nervous and quiet. Even though I love Jesus and want others to know Him, I can find witnessing uncomfortable and scary. So back to WWSD. As I entered my local flower/gift store two weeks ago, that is exactly what popped into my head when I saw the cash register lady. Instead of just buying what I needed and hurrying back home to work, I stopped and thought, "What would Sally do in this situation?"

Then I used an opening line I have often heard Sally say, "What do you do besides work here?" What followed was a beautiful opportunity to listen to this lady share her story, which opened the door for me to share my own story and how amazing it is to live in relationship with Jesus. I was able to share how it is not about religion and rules, but rather receiving God's love and grace. I was able to pray for her at the end and give her an encouraging word. She was so touched that her countenance transformed before my eyes. Why? Because she encountered the love of God in her own workplace. She told me that my coming in that day was serendipitous, as she had needed encouragement.

Sharing God's love with others doesn't have to be difficult or scary. It can become part of your daily life by using everyday moments to bless others. This is what I have learned from years of watching Sally, whom I also have the privilege of calling my mother. She uses every opportunity: from the good to the difficult and inconvenient. She even uses suffering and the loss of her husband, my father, to share God's Love and Truth with others. For years she has prayed daily for God to empower her with His Holy Spirit to be bold so that she could be His Ambassador wherever she goes.

Empowered Faith is a book filled with stories of Sally sowing seeds of love and truth in everyday life. Some of the stories will make you laugh, and others might make you cry. But more than just an inspirational book of one person's faith in action, this book is an activation for you, the reader, to have bolder faith. The Holy Spirit wants to empower you to move outside your comfort zone, to see mishaps as opportunities to witness, and to recognize that God wants to move through you to bless others in ordinary everyday ways.

– Jennifer Miller

Founder, Prosper Always

Introduction

There is power available to all believers to do what Jesus did. Throughout His life on earth Jesus modeled how to live a life of love, caring for those around us. Hear these incredible words He spoke to His disciples, "Truly I say to you, if anyone has faith in me, He will do what I have been doing. He will do even greater things than these because I am going to the Father" (John 14:12). Is it possible? To do greater things? Jesus ministered to sinners' hearts. He healed the sick and set captives free. Can we? Yes! By the empowerment of the Holy Spirit, who is the blessed gift from God enabling us to accomplish God's purposes. With emboldened faith, we can do what Jesus asked of us.

Let your light shine before men.

Go and preach the Gospel

Love your neighbor as yourself.

Do unto others as you would have them do to you.

Abide in me and bear much fruit for the glory of God.

Matthew 5:16, Mark 16:15, Matthew 22:39, Luke 6:31, John 15:5

These are familiar verses but if we honestly examine our hearts, how well do we live this out? There is a harvest field beyond the door of our hearts and homes. Might God be calling us to spend time in this field? Years ago, the revelation that my life is not my own began to break into my self-directed life, causing me to question, "How well am I following Jesus?"

A truth Paul spoke to the believers in Corinth caused my heart to rethink my walk with Jesus: "For the love of Christ compels me, for we are convinced that one died for all, therefore all died. That those who live should no longer live for themselves, but for Him who died for them" (2 Corinthians 5:14-15). I began to reflect on how I was living my life as a pastor's wife and ministry leader and wondered if I could do better at following Jesus and being His witness in this world. Truth be told, though I was involved in various ministries, I wasn't doing much to share my faith with those I encountered day to day who might not know Christ. My prayer became what our Lord asked of us in these verses: "I tell you, open your eyes and look at the fields! They are ripe for harvest" (John 4: 35). "The harvest is plentiful, but the workers are few. Ask the Lord of the harvest, therefore, to send out workers into His harvest field" (Luke 10:2). I was burdened by the reality that in the past four decades of my Christian walk, I have hardly ever had someone witness to me and share their faith.

We may not all be called to be like Billy Graham, but could we perhaps sow seeds along the path of life to bless others? Consider with me what this may look like: "A sower went out to sow his seed." A Bible passage from the Gospel of Luke (8:5) brings us a story that used common imagery for those living in the first century. Put yourself in another day and time, a simpler time, and consider this metaphor for what could be one of the purposes of life on planet earth. Ponder the idea that every day we have the opportunity to sow seeds. These seeds could be sharing a compliment, offering a prayer, or giving out a Bible verse or word of encouragement. What kind of seeds do we sow? What kind of fruit is coming forth? What harvest might we look forward to? Like Jesus, may we allow God's Spirit to equip us to sow seeds as a way of being His witness, trusting that God will water and nurture the seed that faith would grow. We can make a difference in the harvest fields surrounding us—in our family, neighborhood, workplace, city, and even our nation.

Life empowered by the Holy Spirit can be a joyful adventure! This book is meant to encourage, inspire, and activate readers to become seed sowers. I share true life stories from the past fifteen years as I have practiced being the light of Christ wherever I go—sharing God's love and Biblical truth with a world longing for eternal meaning. "The grass withers, the flowers fade, but the Word of God will last forever" (Isaiah 40:8). Jesus loves to see His sons and daughters live in faith, availing ourselves of the power He has given us by His Spirit to be His witnesses in our world. How incredibly interesting it is to awake each day wondering what God has in store as we allow Him to direct our steps. Our lives are not our own; we belong to Christ and His leadership over our lives is beautiful and perfect. How blessed our lives are as we seek to bring Him glory and to see life as a Spirit-led journey of faith. Are you ready for adventure and blessing as a seed sower? Read on.

The Parable of the Sower

A farmer went out to sow his seed. As he was scattering the seed, some fell along the path, and the birds came and ate it up. Some fell on rocky places, where it did not have much soil. It sprang up quickly, because the soil was shallow. But when the sun came up, the plants were scorched, and they withered because they had no root. Other seed fell among thorns, which grew up and choked the plants. Still other seed fell on good soil, where it produced a crop—a hundred, sixty or thirty times what was sown. Whoever has ears, let them hear.

Listen then to what the parable of the sower means: When anyone hears the message about the kingdom and does not understand it, the evil one comes and snatches away what was sown in their heart. This is the seed sown along the path. The seed falling on rocky ground refers to someone who hears the word and at once receives it with joy. But since they have no root, they last only a short time. When trouble or persecution comes because of the word, they quickly fall away. The seed falling among the thorns refers to someone who hears the word, but the worries of this life and the deceitfulness of wealth choke the word, making it unfruitful. But the seed falling on good soil refers to someone who hears the word and understands it. This is the one who produces a crop, yielding a hundred, sixty, or thirty times what was sown.

Matthew 13:3-9, 18-23

1

The Power of the Gospel

I am not ashamed of the Gospel, because it is the power of God for the salvation of everyone who believes: first for the Jew, then for the Gentiles. For in the Gospel the righteousness from God is revealed, a righteousness that is by faith.

Romans 1:16-17

Heard any good news lately? Probably not. Daily we're exposed to a profusion of bad news from our various media sources, but how refreshing to receive good news. Christianity is a religion of good news. From the beginning it was revealed as the Gospel of Jesus Christ. The word Gospel comes from the old English "Godspell," meaning "good story" or "good news" and referring to the good news that God provides through Jesus Christ who brought salvation to the world by His life, death, and resurrection. Jesus Christ was born in human likeness yet lived a sinless life. He offered His life as a perfect sacrifice to pay the penalty for sin. He came as a servant, obedient to His Father and willing to suffer: walking in perfect humility, bringing the good news of salvation, healing the sick, and delivering people from bondage.

The good news concerning Jesus Christ is beautifully revealed in the well-known verse found in the Gospel of John chapter 3, verse 16. "For God so loved the world that He gave His only Son that whoever believes in Him should not perish but have everlasting life." For those of us who have received this good news and walk as followers of Jesus Christ we now seek to live as He lived. Which means there are many opportunities that come to us in everyday life if we have eyes to see these Divine setups, and if we allow God's Spirit to lead us to share our faith and speak through us. What a privilege to share the good news and observe beautiful transformations in individuals as we speak the wonderful words of new life In Christ. It always amazes me to watch the Holy Spirit move in hearts—whether resistant at first or open and hungry for the Gospel.

For some practical help for those who want to know how to go about sharing their faith, sowing good seeds in daily life but aren't certain how to do it, I offer the following. Foremost, in order to be effective witnesses, we need the power of the Holy Spirit. In Acts 1:8 we have this exhortation: "You shall receive power when the Holy Spirit comes upon you and you will be my witnesses ..." For my first twenty-five years serving with my husband Alan in ministry I was timid, and my introverted nature made it hard to talk with strangers. I prayed and prayed for the Holy Spirit to give me boldness. In 2008, I attended Global Awakening's nine-month School of Ministry and during that year, my prayer was gradually answered, and I received empowerment to share my faith, talk with strangers, and present the Gospel (good news) of Jesus Christ. Something wonderful had happened, thanks be to God.

Secondly, I found it much easier to talk about faith and a relationship with Jesus Christ by presenting my own Scripture handouts which I still carry with me in my purse. I know there are some who are comfortable with sharing published Gospel tracts, but for me it was easier to give out my own. Here's what I say as I'm checking out in a grocery store: "Hey, I'm a person of faith and prayer and I love to bless and encourage people. I have these blessing prayers (or Scriptures) I'd like to share with you." In giving them out I may only have one or two minutes in conversation, so I may quickly share my testimony of how I came to have faith in Jesus Christ. If I'm in a waiting room or on an airplane, I may have fifteen minutes or even an hour for spiritual conversation. One of my lead-in sentences after a few minutes of casual talk may be, "Hey, I'm a person of faith. Where are you in your spiritual life?" This extra time will enable you to go into more detail about living a life of faith and what it's like to have a relationship with Father God and His Son Jesus. Memorizing Scripture is immensely helpful to have truth readily available to offer as hope and encouragement. Another handout I use is titled, "God is Our Strength in Time of Need." It includes verses on trust, peace and hope. Consider compiling your own list of favorite verses and printing them on nice paper that you carry with you allowing you to sow the seed of God's Word. I have sat next to numerous people on airplanes who upon receiving Scripture handouts will then spend 5-10 minutes reading it and usually thank me after.

God's word is powerful and transforming. With this simple act, you can make a difference in someone's life, even for eternity.

My third recommendation is to pray regularly, asking the Holy Spirit to show you how He can use you as His witness and to lead you. One of my frequent prayers is one of yielding: "Holy Spirit, fill me, use me. Jesus, live Your life through me." Ask that God would direct you daily to an individual He wants you to encounter so that you might share the Gospel. In time we become attuned to the leading of the Spirit as we seek to follow Him, and He directs our steps. "How beautiful on the mountains are the feet of those who bring good news, who proclaim peace, who bring good tidings" (Isaiah 52:7).

❦

Sowing the Seeds of the Gospel

However, I consider my life worth nothing to me, if only I may finish the race and complete the task the Lord Jesus has given to me, the task of testifying to the Gospel of God's grace. Acts 20:24

Yet when I preach, I cannot boast, for I am compelled to preach. Woe to me if I do not preach the Gospel. 1 Corinthians 9:16

The God of this age has blinded the minds of unbelievers, so that they cannot see the light of the Gospel of the glory of Christ, who is the image of God. For we do not preach ourselves, but Jesus Christ as Lord, and ourselves as your servants for Jesus' sake. For God, who said, "Let light shine out of darkness," made His light shine in our hearts to give us the light of the knowledge of the glory of God in the face of Christ. 2 Corinthians 4:4-6

All over the world this Gospel is bearing fruit and growing, just as it has been doing among you since the day you heard it and understood God's grace and all its truth. Colossians 1:6

But join me with suffering for the Gospel, by the power of God, who has saved us and called us to a holy life—not because of anything we have done, but because of his own purpose and grace. This grace was given us in Christ Jesus before the beginning of time, but it has now been revealed through the appearing of our savior Jesus Christ, who has destroyed death and brought life and immortality to light through the Gospel. 2 Timothy 1:8b-10

Isaac's Restaurant —Mechanicsburg, Pennsylvania (June 2014)

During the 2014 Global Awakening conference Alan and I went to Isaac's restaurant and met our server, Peter. We started engaging him in conversation and told him about the conference and about God still speaking today with words of prophecy. We shared that we felt he was a man of honor and that God's desire was to restore him and bring him into his destiny, bringing his dreams to life. We asked him where he was spiritually, and he said he's an atheist.

I said, "Well, I think God wants to change that. I believe God is speaking to you to reveal truth." At first, Peter seemed a little uncomfortable, but then when he returned a second time to our table, we engaged him in further conversation. He explained that 2013 was a difficult year as he had been married thirteen years and now was divorced. I told him this year God wants to restore many things and heal hearts from soul wounds. As I spoke, he was actually leaning forward, listening intently to what I was speaking as God was giving me life-giving words to share with him. He seemed hungry for truth. We prayed for him that God would water the seeds that He let us sow into Peter's life.

❧

Airplane Ministry with Seatmate — Enroute to Ohio (March 23, 2020)

I boarded the plane flying to my daughter Jennifer's home, pleasantly surprised to have a seatmate. The plane had maybe only twenty-five people, as it was the week after the start of the Covid lockdown. There were many empty rows and seats and yet God arranged for me to have a seatmate: Bing Xuhan from China, a student finishing college who was going back to Beijing because of the virus. As we were taking off, I shared with her the Scripture handout "Do Not Fear" that God had led me to compile. She read through it the next ten minutes.

Maybe thirty minutes later, I engaged her again in conversation and shared the prayers for women I had in my purse. She again spent five to ten minutes reading over that sheet. Having talked with a friend the day before about purposing to share the Gospel, I was able to share the Good News of salvation with her, explaining sin and mankind's fall from grace and who Jesus is and why He died on the cross. I told her about eternal life and His resurrection from the dead and the Holy Spirit's power given to those who believe and receive Christ. She was so open! Oh, praise the Lord! How wonderful to share the Good News. I asked if she'd like a copy of my book, Out of Suffering into Glory and gave her a PDF of it. Praise You, Lord, for answering my prayer to be intentional in sharing Jesus and His way of salvation.

Five Hour Drive = 1 Soul Enters the Kingdom – Clear Lake, Iowa (September 7, 2021)

I was taking a ministry trip to share my Gospel raps and my testimony at Agape Christian Family Church in Clear Lake, Iowa, a quaint town Alan and I had visited in 2017. It was a somewhat challenging time as I was taking this trip alone, and it was one and a half years after Alan went home to be with the Lord. On one of the days there, I felt the Holy Spirit leading me to visit a lovely garden which Alan and I had visited on our last trip. When I entered the garden, I saw a young woman and her dog sitting on a bench. I wanted to talk to her and used the excuse of commenting about her beautiful Alaskan Malamute dog.

We talked casually for a few minutes, and I began to share my faith with her. My heart was touched when I heard her story—that she had evacuated recently from Louisiana because of Hurricane Ida. We spoke together for a long time and I learned she had been through a lot in her life. I shared my testimony: briefly explaining the trials and hardship in my early life. I kept pointing her to Jesus and the Holy Spirit and the incredible difference having faith has made in my life the past forty-five years. I explained that she could pray and ask Jesus into her life. I shared that if we confess our sins and ask for God's forgiveness, He will forgive us and we become a child of God made right in His sight. She prayed with me, and a new child entered the Kingdom of God. Praise the Lord! Jesus, how amazing that perhaps this five-hour trip was for reaching this lost daughter of Yours.

⸎

Coffee Shop – Waterville, Ohio (December 28, 2022)

I had flown to Ohio to spend Christmas with my daughter's family. I planned to meet a friend in a local coffee shop a few days after Christmas. I didn't check my text prior to driving to the coffee shop, but while I was waiting, I looked at my texts and saw that my friend had canceled at the last minute for a work situation. So, there I was in the coffee shop alone. Was this a Divine setup?

I looked around the café and saw several couples, and then I saw a woman sitting alone. "OK, God, should I go up and introduce myself?" The Holy Spirit gave me boldness, and I walked over to her.

"Hi, I was supposed to meet a friend here, but she canceled at the last minute. I'm a person of faith and prayer, and I have this Christmas handout that I've been sharing with people to bless them. I put together verses on God's gifts to us in this season of giving." (On the handout the first one is God's gift of His Son Jesus given to us at Christmas.)

She said, "I could use a blessing." I kept talking and briefly shared my testimony as I was standing at her table. I shared that there's a lot of anxiety and depression in our nation that has been increasing the past few years, and God offers hope and desires to help us. He wants us to turn to him. Also, I told her that I have a Gospel rap on YouTube and love to share it with young people who are especially struggling these days.

She agreed and said, "Yeah, my kids are having a hard time." I told her where she could find it on my website. At this point her friend showed up. When I told the friend what we had been talking about, she said, "That was a God-setup."

God redeemed the canceled meeting with my friend so that I could share the Good News with Esme. Amazing that this encounter with Esme wouldn't have happened if my friend had showed up. Thank you, God, that You turn things around for good and for Your purposes.

Prayer

God our Father, thank You for giving Your Son, Jesus Christ, to save sinners. We were lost and in darkness—not even aware of our need to be reconciled to You. Thank You that Jesus came to earth bringing light and truth, revealing Your love and passionate desire to bring us into relationship with You through the forgiveness of our sins. We are Your children, created in Your image, and made for fullness of life. Jesus our Savior, thank You that You died in our place, taking the punishment we deserved, bringing us peace. We are delivered out of the darkness into Your light and in You we have purpose, love, and joy. You alone are "the Way, the Truth, and the Life. No one comes to the Father except through You" (John 14:6). May we live in humility, following Your example and sharing the Good News of the Gospel with family, friends, and those around us. Thank You that Your Spirit gives us boldness to make You known. May we always be ready to present the invitation to turn from sin, receive Your forgiveness, and accept the free gift of righteousness. How grateful we are for the blessed assurance of eternal life through Christ. Amen.

2

God of the Broken Bumper

*The Spirit of the Sovereign Lord is on me, because the
Lord has anointed me to proclaim good news to the poor. He
has sent me to bind up the brokenhearted, to proclaim freedom
for the captives and release from darkness for the prisoners.*

Isaiah 61:1

I think an angel did it—on assignment from the God of the
Universe. I backed my van out of our narrow fifty-year-old
garage, just as I did every day, but that one summer day . . . crunch!
Metal scraping metal as my bumper was broken off. The full story and
what resulted is coming up.

Life on our planet earth is fragile; we live in a broken world. So
much brokenness exists in our material world and in the internal
world of relationships and soul life. I had a season a few years ago
where I seemed to be at war with gravity. Glasses, plates, a jar of olives
all succumbed to gravity and set me up for the choice between two
emotional responses. I could resort to anger, frustration, and some
choice word from my pre-Christian days, or I could laugh, get the
broom, and say, "Praise the Lord anyway." The latter response was my
husband's tool against frustration which was based on Paul's word to
the church in Thessalonica: "Give thanks in all circumstances for this
is God's will for you in Christ Jesus" (1 Thessalonians 5:18). Getting
back to the brokenness theme—things on earth just don't last forever.
Might there be a redemptive purpose for brokenness? How does
empowered faith face the brokenness here on planet earth?

Life presents many challenges to our mental, emotional, and spiritual well-being as we experience broken bodies, broken marriages, broken hopes and dreams, broken hearts, etc. The result is obvious—pain, disappointment, and sorrow. In looking at passages from God's Word we read of Jesus healing broken bodies, restoring hearts that have been broken, and demonstrating His great love for humankind. Might we consider bringing to Jesus as an offering the brokenness that touches our inner being or the material things we hold too tightly? Could we see Him glorified through our brokenness?

As I've journeyed through life, I have come to trust God for His ability to use broken things in a way that redeems the hardship. I have seen Jesus, my comforter and friend, heal my broken heart after the death of my mother when I was only seven years old and my father when I was twenty-five. He understands suffering and witnessed the brokenness of those on earth. Out of profound love and compassion, He touched bodies and souls bringing wholeness. And so, through Jesus, brokenness can be a starting point and not the end of the journey for our lives on earth. And as we journey, we may be given opportunities to sow compassion, kindness and God's love. Brokenness can rightly cause us to feel many emotions, but in God's hands and by His sovereign will, there is purpose that one day will be revealed.

From the world of art a meaningful metaphor is given to us where brokenness can lead to something even more beautiful. Kintsugi is the Japanese art form of using gold to repair broken pottery pieces in which the flaws and imperfections create a more stunning work of art. From the brokenness of life, maturity comes and faith grows as we allow God to redeem our pain. In a time of personal healing a few years ago, God accomplished something similar. He showed me the broken foundation of my life, but I saw the golden glory of His love, pouring into my life to restore and heal and strengthen my inner being, allowing the overflow of love to touch hurting individuals He brings into my life.

Consider how the following verses reflect God's view of brokenness and may the testimonies shared bring new awareness and fresh perspective to your life and the doors that may open for sowing seeds from your empowered faith.

Sowing Seeds Through Brokenness

Broken loaves feed multitudes.

When he had taken the seven loaves and given thanks, he broke them and gave them to his disciples to distribute to the people. Mark 8:6-9

Broken bodies reveal the Divine Healer.

So, he said to the paralyzed man, "I tell you, get up, take your mat and go home." Immediately he stood up in front of them, took what he had been lying on and went home praising God. Everyone was amazed and gave praise to God. Luke 5:17-25

A broken alabaster jar anointed the Son of God.

A woman came with an alabaster jar of very expensive perfume, made of pure nard. She broke the jar and poured the perfume on his head. Mark 14:3

A broken body of our Lord was given for us.

While they were eating, Jesus took bread, and when he had given thanks, He broke it and gave it to his disciples, saying, "Take it; this is my body given for you." Mark 14:2

Broken hearts mend because of the good news.

The Spirit of the Sovereign Lord is on me, because the Lord has anointed me to proclaim good news to the poor. He has sent me to bind up the brokenhearted, to proclaim freedom for the captives and release from darkness for the prisoners. Isaiah 61:1

Broken Bumper Leads to Worship — Grandview, Missouri (July 2015)

Backing my van out of our narrow fifty-year-old garage one pleasant summer day. . . crunch! What happened? How could this be? What was different that day in getting the van out of the garage? Oh no! So, the wife prayed before telling her husband, so he won't get upset. "Lord, I praise you and thank you that All things work together for good for those who love God and are called for His purpose like it says in Romans 8:28."

I chose to offer God extravagant worship rather than giving the enemy any credit for the mishap with the van. (It really is a very narrow garage, and I really am a good driver.) I took time thanking God for all things, praising Him, worshiping Him and refused to get upset, trusting that God allowed this and has His purposes for ALL things. I got the victory; my heart was trusting. Then I told the husband and he also said, "Praise the Lord anyway. That's what insurance is for." (What a great husband!)

The next day I took the van to a garage to have them reattach the bumper. I sat in the waiting room and met Kevin, a seventeen-year-old high school student. I quickly got into God talk, told how great it is to walk with Jesus, and shared stories for ten minutes of how God speaks to us—including Alan's testimony from his book of hearing God's voice during Desert Storm in 1991 which led to lives being saved. I shared the testimony of my husband Alan's former boss, US Senate Chaplain Barry Black, who was taught by his mother to memorize God's Word that saved his life as he heard God warn him not to go with gang members who ended up killing a man. They went to prison. Chaplain Black went on to become a Navy Admiral and US Senate Chaplain. Kevin was enthralled and said, "I've gotta get your husband's book!" I told him Alan's book Take Charge of Your Destiny is on Amazon. He said, "I'm definitely going to read it."

I went over and shook his hand and prayed for him in the waiting room—for God to be revealed to him and for Kevin to hear God's voice and let Him direct Kevin's steps. Praise the Lord! God had a reason for allowing the bumper to get ripped off. (I still think an angel did it.)

Lord, thank You for the privilege of sharing God stories with those we encounter daily. We pray that Kevin and others searching like him would come to know You and allow Christ into their lives. Open their hearts, their eyes, and their minds to Your greatness. Amen!

‿ぐ⚭ン‿

Broken Purse Leads to Salvation – Carlisle, Pennsylvania (November 17, 2017)

I was visiting friends in Pennsylvania and, while there, bought a new purse at JC Penny's. The next day the zipper broke. Ugh! "Oh, no. Hmm, maybe You're setting up a Divine assignment, God."

So, the next day I went back to exchange it. A young woman was sitting outside the mall, and I felt led to talk with her. "Hi, how's your day going?" She shared a little and then I started sharing about God's love and faith in Jesus and how I love to encourage people in walking in faith. She seemed open but shared she wasn't too spiritual. I told her I rap about God's love and asked if I could share it.

"Wow!" she said when the rap was finished. I told her about how amazing Jesus is—that He's our living Savior and He came to restore us to a relationship with Father God. He died in our place for the things we do wrong and through repentance, wants to give us true life as we are born again by the Spirit. His life is the source of perfect love, perfect peace, and perfect joy.

Terry was so thirsty! I had been praying the past six months that I not only wanted to plant seeds, but I also wanted to see a harvest! I want to lead people to Jesus! Terry was very open. So, I took the next step and broke through the barrier that's kept me these past years from leading people to salvation. I asked if I could pray with her, if she wanted to ask Jesus into her life and she said, "Yes I guess so." So, I prayed sentence by sentence and she repeated after me, asking Jesus to forgive her sins and to be her Savior, and inviting the Holy Spirit to live in her. Yay God! I told her that there's a party in Heaven now as the Bible says angels rejoice when people come to know Jesus.

I got my book from my van and showed her some Bible verses and told her the first chapters in my book would answer a lot of questions she may have. I also told her how important it is to read the Bible. Praise the Lord! My heart was full of joy in this breakthrough that the Spirit helped me to lead someone to Christ. I had been bold to pray with people and share the Lord in the past, but had always hesitated to have them pray the sinner's prayer. Well, hallelujah! Thank you, Jesus! I then went into the store to exchange the purse, and then I went back to the van with tears of joy.

Pray for Terry and those who are broken—that God would nurture them and help them grow in faith, that the Holy Spirit would reveal God's love and establish them on Christ the Rock of Salvation.

$$\sim\!\!\sim\!\!\ast\!\!\sim\!\!\sim$$

Bike Riding Accident – Longview Lake, Missouri (August 2017)

Well, it began as a pleasant day riding bikes on a trail at a nearby lake. I was in front of my husband Alan and saw ruts on the trail ahead. I turned to warn him to be careful and ugh, the rut took me down. Crash. OK still in one piece, but I thought my arm was broken. Ow! So painful!

Alan's like, "Get up, and I'll help you walk back to the van."

And I'm like, "No. I'm gonna puke or faint. Let me lie down in the dirt here."

Quite concerned, Alan called 911 and an ambulance came in eight minutes. On the way to the ER they gave me morphine and I started to feel oh so good. Then I had a sudden revelation: "Oh, it's a Divine assignment!" So, I started witnessing to the two men about Jesus.

One guy quickly moved up front, leaving me with Jason. I asked about his faith, but he said he was not too religious. I shared my testimony and that perhaps God wanted me to share with him about how amazing Jesus is and that this happened to put me in his ambulance to encourage him spiritually. He was listening attentively. The Spirit was opening his heart. God was touching him. We got to the ER and thankfully my arm was not broken, just bruised and sprained. I wore a sling for four days and slowly the arm healed.

Lord, thank you for using this incident to put me with Jason to sow seeds of the good news of the life-giving relationship we can have with Jesus.

Army Sniper and Plumber — Grandview, Missouri (January 29, 2016)

Don't be surprised when your phone stops working, and the washing machine breaks—

Jehovah Sneaky is at work. The phone repairman came, and Alan and I found out he was a former Army sniper. Alan started talking about God, and after resolving the issue with the phone, we asked if we could pray for him. He had shared that he had received multiple injuries during his Army deployments, so we prayed and the Lord touched him.

Then a few days later we had to call the plumber to look at our washing machine. It was another God set-up and this man also received prayer after being asked where he was with Jesus. He was open to hearing about a personal relationship with Christ and we prayed God's blessing upon him, his work, and his family, and that he would grow in faith.

Marriage Vows Broken — Arlington, Virginia (Spring 2005)

The most painful aspect of brokenness often comes from those relationships closest to us. In 2005, we received a call from our heartbroken daughter Jennifer that her husband of eight years had left her and wanted a divorce. Through tears and anguish, the situation unfolded in her life that is all too familiar to many in our nation. Her marriage was broken—she was abandoned, deserted by the one who had vowed to remain by her side.

It was a time of great pain for all of us in our family, yet it also became a time of watching God do something amazing in our daughter. He comforted her, brought her strength, and renewed her faith even in her suffering. In one of her darkest moments, she was reminded of Ephesians 3:20. "Now to him who is able to do exceedingly abundantly above all that we ask or think, according to the power that works in us."

In this trial Jennifer turned to Jesus with her broken heart to find consolation in the grief of her abandonment. God's Word became her lifeline as she sought God's face, even praying through the book of Psalms over a weekend personal retreat. The promises came into her soul from the Heart-mender. "He heals the brokenhearted and binds up their wounds" (Psalm 147:3). Jennifer received the Holy Spirit's inner healing, peace, joy, and the awareness that she was not alone. God would not forsake her, and she could trust Jesus for her deepest needs to be met.

Jennifer has become a powerful woman of God through her suffering. In spite of the eventual divorce, she allowed God's grace to work deeply in her heart. She wrote a letter forgiving her ex-husband, choosing to trust God for her future, and not allowing any root of bitterness to form. With God's help, she moved on with her life. Three years after her divorce God brought a godly man into her life who had been waiting on God for his life partner. She and Jason have now been married many years and have two wonderful children, Lily and Zachary.

Prayer

God of the broken bumper and God who heals broken hearts, thank You for Your love, Your kindness, Your presence with us in times of brokenness. Give me new understanding in how to view life when presented with challenges. When material things break, may I let go, realizing that You want me to hold lightly to the things of this world, but hold tightly to You. On a deeper level, You are the One who takes broken bodies, broken relationships, broken dreams, and broken hearts and will use them for Your glory. Let me see Your Divine set-ups in day-to-day life, so I can bless those around me. You make things beautiful in Your time. Amen.

3

Rapping for Jesus
Being a Fool for Christ

Always be prepared to give an answer to everyone who asks you to give the reason for the hope that you have.

1 Peter 3:15

A rapper for Jesus? I'm blonde, I'm white, and I'm seventy: not your typical rapper. I don't remember how it started except I enjoy being creative with words. I'm a wordsmith, I suppose. My passion is to share in whatever way possible the good news of salvation, of forgiveness of sins and the abundant life believers have through Jesus Christ. Paul the Apostle of Jesus described his method to win others to Christ with these impassioned words: "To the Jews I become like a Jew to win the Jews … to the weak I become weak to win the weak. I have become all things to all men so that by all possible means I might save some" (1 Corinthians 9:20, 22).

God put that same desire in my heart so that I am willing to be a fool for Christ. Rapping from a blond senior looks pretty foolish to the generation I'm trying to reach. I am almost always greeted with laughter when I tell people, "Hey, I love to share about God's love. He's given me a rap—can I share it with you?" Laughter disarms my listeners. My rap, which might look foolish, has become a key that opens hearts.

In 2017 I was desperate for a way to present life-changing truth to those I encounter. Out of the tragic loss of two young nephews in my husband's family, I was moved to pray for the Holy Spirit to give me words that speak life to the younger generation. Surprisingly the answer came as two raps. For the first one, I started to have Bible verses come into my thoughts and then I arranged words creatively for a rhyme and beat. This resulted in a "Scripture Rap," which presents the truth from God's Word in powerful declarations. A year later I sought God for a second rap that would present the Gospel clearly and would have the Holy Spirit's empowerment. My prayer was answered as words and stanzas came through Divine inspiration. God downloaded to me a beautiful invitation from His heart to touch the souls of my listeners.

Jesus didn't rap but He used parables to reach the generation of His day. Parables of sowing seeds, of fishing nets, of hidden treasure, of lost sheep. He used these illustrative stories to capture the hearts and minds of His listeners. I rap to capture the hearts and minds of my listeners who, out of curiosity, become very attentive as the Lord gives me an opening that I share in airports, parks, stores, and waiting rooms. They listen to see if this lady can "spit some bars," a rap term meaning the words are impactful and skillfully rhyme. One stranger named Michael with whom I shared the rap, was the first to share this, as he couldn't believe what he was hearing and even said, "Those are some powerful words!"

I've included the words of my "Jesus Rap" and stories of how I use the rap to make connections with others, seeing God open hearts, and pointing them to Jesus.

See it on Youtube: Sally's rap.
https://www.youtube.com/watch?v=MPPs-euadwQ

JESUS RAP
(God's Heart for You)

You search for it high—you search for it low

Wherever you search He'll also go

There's an inner longing—it's been there from the start

He knows cuz He put it there—It's from his own heart

Peace, purpose—to know that you're loved

It's through an open doorway sent from above

Some may say it's narrow—to some it's just too hard

But it's the one way given and choosing brings reward

Walk through the doorway—it's the path of grace

Your sins forgiven, your guilt erased

It's the way of freedom—truth has a Name

Jesus the Lord—the world His domain

The Way, the Truth—He is the Life.

Overcoming strongholds and every form of strife

He gives Living Water—to quench every thirst

Reach for His cup—yes, drink it first

It's a cup of Love—a Fountain of Grace

No longer afraid to see your Father's face

He's your true Father—He'll never cause pain

Every spiritual blessing for your eternal gain

To Him belongs all glory—He's worthy of our praise

We're made for His pleasure—to love Him all our days

To stand before His presence—no fear no guilt no shame

Perfect Love embracing you—True Life in Jesus Name

Sowing Seeds Through the Spoken Word

By the Word of the Lord the heavens were made, their starry host by the breath of His mouth … Let all the earth fear the Lord; let all the people of the world revere Him. For He Spoke, and it came to be; He commanded, and it stood firm. Psalm 33:6-9

The Spirit gives life; the flesh counts for nothing. The Words I have spoken to you—they are full of the Spirit and Life. John 6:63

But in these last days He has spoken to us by His Son, whom He appointed the heir of all things, through whom also He created the world. Hebrews 1:2

It is written: "I believed; therefore I have spoken." Since we have that same spirit of faith, we also believe and therefore speak. 2 Corinthians 4:13

For prophecy never had its origin in the human will, but prophets, though human, spoke from God as they were carried along by the Holy Spirit. 2 Peter 1:21

Because of my trial, most of the brothers and sisters have been encouraged to speak the Word of God more courageously and fearlessly. Philippians 1:14

Mourning to Joy – Arlington National Cemetery – Washington DC (September 8, 2022)

I arrived on our anniversary at Alan's grave and immediately began to cry. I was with Lisa Schultz, who took his place as Chief of Staff for U. S. Senate Chaplain Barry Black. Through my tears I spoke to Jesus thanking Him for giving me this amazing husband for forty-six years. As tears flowed two small vehicles—a tractor and a small truck carrying a casket and seven men arrived in the vicinity.

A man walked up and told us that we needed to leave for a time as they couldn't have us nearby as they were interring a casket near us. Incredulous, I told them I just arrived from Kansas City and was only there for five minutes. I was in the middle of crying, grieving for my husband, "You've got to be kidding." Anger arose in me—the man apologized and said sorry, but we had to go over to the pavilion across the road and wait there and they would do their best to be finished in twenty minutes.

Still, I could not believe this was happening, and said, "Can't you wait for me, since I just arrived at his gravesite?" He was insistent that they have eight funerals a day and he was sorry, but they had to proceed.

Lisa and I walked over to the pavilion as I continued to sob now. Not believing this was happening. As I sat there crying, I thought, "Wait a minute!" I remembered my recent teaching with "witnesses" as an acrostic:

Whatever

Inconveniences

To

Normal

Everyday

Schedule

Surrender

Everything to the

Spirit who empowers us

I told Lisa this and then began to laugh as I thought, "Oh, all right, this is inconvenient and an interruption to what I thought was going to happen this morning." I asked Jesus why He allowed this, but already my spirit was anticipating His answer.

I looked at the seven men gathered near Alan's grave site, working to put to rest another veteran. I told Lisa, "Let's just flip this around and use this opportunity to pray for these men." Who knows? There might be something serious going on in one of their lives, and God was giving us an opportunity to bless them. We began to pray—for God's love to come upon them, for His grace, kindness and mercy to touch their lives, for their families and marriages, for addictions to be broken off and salvation, etc. My attitude totally changed.

Lisa was surprised how I turned it around and that this was how I've been seeing life lately: allowing God to interrupt what I think my plans should be and instead showing me His plans. So, we continued to laugh a bit about this. Then Holy Spirit boldness came on me and I went up to the first man who had spoken to us and apologized and told him Alan had been a Navy Chaplain. "We're people of faith and we're praying God's blessing on you all." Then I went up to two other men and shared the same.

Fifteen minutes later, we could tell the men were finishing up at the gravesite. Only four were left and suddenly Holy Spirit boldness came on me again and we went over to them. I told them who Alan was and how he loved people and would have shared his faith in Jesus Christ and thoughts of eternity and how we need Jesus. I told them that I rapped, and they all laughed a bit but decided to show them a line or two … which turned into doing the whole rap for them. One guy began to beatbox with me and all of them were smiling. There I was near Alan's grave with these cemetery workers, sharing the "Jesus Rap."

I felt the Holy Spirit all over this visit turning my "mourning into laughter and sorrow into joy" (Jeremiah 31). Alan would have been witnessing to them and God allowed me to carry on his legacy. This truth came to me from John 12:24, "I tell you the truth, unless a kernel of wheat is planted in the soil and dies, it remains alone. But its death will produce many new kernels—a plentiful harvest of new lives."

We did go over to the grave after everyone had gone, and I had time to reflect and remember this amazing man God gave me for forty-six years of marriage. God didn't want me to cry and interrupted my mourning. Sadness to joy! We prayed before we departed from Arlington National Cemetery–for our nation, for revival, for spiritual awakening and for the Spirit to pour out on our land.

May my husband Alan's legacy be released in and through your life—to love those around you, to be witnesses of God's saving grace, to have Holy Spirit boldness to share Jesus in your daily life, to fulfill your destiny on earth while bringing God glory. God is so good!

Roaring River Resort – Ozarks, Arkansas (May 30, 2018)

On vacation in the Ozarks, we were getting ready to leave and felt led to stop at Roaring River Resort. Their signboard quoted a Bible verse, so we assumed the owners were Christian. Crystal, a young woman, worked for them and said that the owners were strong Christians and she was a Christian also. We got information about the cabins and room rates and then got in a spiritual conversation. We commended her for her faith in Christ and shared some God stories with her. Told her about my passion for reaching young people with whatever means, including that God had given me two raps. She seemed surprised and gave me "the look."

At first as I shared my "Jesus Rap" with her, she smiled, almost laughing, probably at how foolish it seemed to see me rapping. Then the Holy Spirit grabbed her heart. It was quite an amazing transformation of her listening intently to the words and receiving the truth from the Holy Spirit satisfying her soul-thirst. She stared as I finished the rap and then said it was beautiful and it touched her. We prayed for her, and Alan spoke into her life. She blessed us by saying that she was so glad she worked that day and had met us.

40 Marines Hear Rap – Dam Neck Naval Base, Virginia Beach, Virginia (June 11, 2024)

I was on a road trip to the East Coast in June of 2024 when I visited the beach at Dam Neck Naval Base, enjoying an early morning walk on the beach. I was driving back to my friend's house and passed the base chapel. I felt led to do a U-turn and go in to say hello to the chaplains, as my husband Alan had been stationed in Virginia Beach almost forty years ago. As I walked in, I saw a group of maybe forty young Marines assembled in the chapel, standing around waiting for something. I walked in and asked if there was a chaplain there and they said no, they were there for graduation from Marine Intelligence Specialist School.

Holy Spirit boldness came on me and I told the several Marines in front of me that I rap, and I was a chaplain's wife who speaks at churches and asked if they'd like to hear a rap. They all smiled and said sure. Then I said, "Can you get the attention of the rest of the group?"

The young marine yelled, "Hey, listen up, this lady wants to rap for us." (He told me they were waiting till 10:00 for the ceremony and it was only 9:30.)

Wow, what a wonderful opportunity. I introduced myself to the whole group of forty assembled, told them my husband had been a Navy chaplain, and that I love to share God's love, sometimes through rap. That got lots of surprised and curious looks. So, I did the "Jesus Rap"—the majority were smiling, moving with the rhythm, enjoying it. Then I commended them for being willing to serve our nation in the military and prayed God's blessing over them, protection, and for their future destiny. I thanked them for letting me share and that it brought me joy as I had lost my husband three years ago from a service-related illness.

CVS Store Employee Divine Assignment – Kansas City, Missouri (April 12, 2019)

In CVS, I hesitated to engage the cashier, a young man, in

conversation. I was tired. But I started talking because he seemed burdened. I asked how he was, and Christian said he wanted to move to Atlanta and was saving up money. I felt led to suggest he pray for direction and to seek God's will. He looked up and became more engaged in conversation. I encouraged him spiritually about God's purposes in our lives and then asked if I could share a rap with him.

Feeling foolish standing there at the CVS counter, I spoke the "Jesus Rap" as he listened intently. Then he said, "I needed that today. God sent you here today." I took his hand feeling the compassion of Jesus and prayed for God's love to touch him, for guidance and blessing. As I walked to the car, tears of gratitude came that I have the honor to make Jesus known and be His vessel of love to the lost and hurting.

⚓

7 Teens, Pool Party and the "Jesus Rap" – Waterville, Ohio (June 17, 2020)

She was leading me by the hand. I was chickening out. I was in Ohio visiting my daughter Jennifer and her family for my granddaughter's birthday. I was staying at an Airbnb, and the neighbor's son had friends over for an afternoon pool party. I had befriended the dad Jerry, who heard my rap, and he invited me over to rap for the boys. Well, I was feeling intimidated by seven teenage boys. But since the dad had asked me to come over, I figured God was in it. So, my granddaughter Lily took me by the hand and led me out the front door. Then the Holy Spirit took over.

The boys sat around a picnic table. I introduced myself and shared that God gave me a couple of raps to express His love to their generation. I prayed for the Holy Spirit to touch them as I shared the rap. They clapped as I finished and then I went on to share my usual stories of how awesome Jesus is and He's given us the Holy Spirit who is supernatural, which makes living our faith very exciting! I gave a few testimonies as they listened. Then I thanked them for letting me share—they were all smiling at me, probably eager to get back in the pool away from this crazy lady. But I asked if I could say a quick prayer for them and blessed them—asking God to reveal His love for them and lead them to have faith and to trust Jesus.

ᕦᕤᕦᕤ

Covid Clinic 4 Staff Hear Gospel – Kansas City, Missouri (May 28, 2021)

At the clinic to get my second covid vaccine I met Darren who checked me in, and I shared the prayers I wrote for men. He was a believer and was encouraged. Then I went back to the room with the nurse. After receiving the vaccine, I shared with her the prayers I wrote for women. I waited fifteen minutes and felt lightheaded, but on my way out I felt God wanted me to tell Darren he was "the son of God's heart," that God was proud of him and pleased that his light was shining.

I felt weak, but Holy Spirit boldness came on me. The waiting room was empty, the four staff people were standing behind the counter. I spoke to Darren about what God had told me. Then the Holy Spirit had me share my faith with the staff and I thought, "Oh no, here it comes. I'm about to be a fool for Christ." Yup, I did my rap for them.

They loved it and all clapped! I gave my testimony and told them how amazing Jesus is. I talked about the power of the Holy Spirit: how wonderful He is, and how Christianity is not boring but exciting. It's an adventure and supernatural. One nurse seemed a little uncomfortable, but the other three staff people told me how I made their day and blessed them. Thank you, Jesus! Amazing that even though I was not at my best after getting the vaccine, I had my prayer answered that I would be a witness for Jesus, and the Kingdom of God manifested in that clinic to bring God glory.

ᕦᕤᕦᕤ

Prayer

Lord, am I willing to be a fool for You? In what ways might You call me to reflect Your love and life to those around me as Your witness? Do I understand that being one of Your witnesses may entail being inconvenienced for You? Help me to remember that whatever inconveniences to normal everyday schedule come, I can surrender everything to the Spirit who empowers me. Am I willing to be laughed at, rejected, and mocked for Your sake? Help me surrender to You my rights, my agenda, my reputation, and my needs so that I would declare with the apostle Paul, "Whatever was to my profit I now consider loss for the sake of Christ. What is more, I consider everything a loss compared to the surpassing greatness of knowing Christ Jesus my Lord" (Philippians 3:7-8). My relationship with You is the most important aspect of my life. Holy Spirit, set my heart on fire that I would desire to sow seeds of love, truth and compassion wherever I go and wherever You lead me. Take my life, Lord, and may it be pleasing to You. In Jesus' name I pray. Amen!

4

Understanding God's Plan for Men

So God created mankind in his own image, in the image
of God he created them; male and female he created them.

Genesis 1:27

I was watching war movies and rescue movies in 2017 and felt moved to tears as I witnessed the courage and sacrifice of men who boldly went into combat ... men who risked their lives to save those in peril ... men who ran into the fire. Tears flowed from deep in my heart creating the desire to express gratitude and admiration for men of courage and integrity. This sentiment gave birth to my handout "Prayers to Bless and Honor Men," which God has used to strengthen and encourage recipients. For five years I have had the privilege of sowing seeds of honor into men I encounter in my everyday life.

What does it mean to honor? It is the respect and esteem shown to one another. As Christians, we are told through Scripture to honor others and show respect. Society in the past exhibited honor and respect more inherently than today. Also, civility, manners, and politeness were taught, and children would grow up to honor their elders. In a school of ministry I recently attended, one of the core values includes a culture of honor: "We intentionally seek to cultivate a culture of honor where we choose to treat one another with the highest regard because they bear the image of God and we celebrate His work in one another's lives. We acknowledge that we can only properly receive from the gifts of others when we honor them."[1]

For some of my readers, this may be a difficult concept to grasp. You may have grown up with a male figure who was hard to respect and honor. After the death of my mom, my dad had two girls to raise and alcohol became his way of dealing with the heavy responsibility. He loved us but at times he would be verbally abusive. I was rebellious in my teen years, but after coming to know Christ in my early twenties, I saw my dad through different eyes and lovingly reaffirmed the Biblical command to love and honor my father. When I forgave him and honored him for doing the best job he was able to do, I became free. I could love my father in spite of his shortcomings, and I could still honor what God intended for fathers to be. A father is meant to protect and love his family and put their needs ahead of his own. If there is a need, ask God to heal your past wounds, so you can honor what male strength is meant to be.

It is apparent that our nation has lost this virtue of honor toward one another: not just in the family, but in government, media, the entertainment industry, in marriages, and even within the church too. Often disrespect and dishonor are shown to others as the norm. As Christians to show honor does not necessarily mean we agree with others in their character and lifestyle, but we value them because they're created in the image of God.

I remember in my childhood men and fathers were honored and esteemed in television shows. However, in the 80s television sitcoms developed a very different family dynamic. Fathers were now out of touch with what was "cool" or were fools compared to the kids, who became the ones to be admired. Also today there can be great disrespect between men and women, causing competition, conflict, and disunity. Remco Brommet explains that men today have to compensate for

[1] *Encounter School of Ministry Handbook,* "Core Values."

the hole in their soul because they have a warrior spirit that has been crushed by modern culture and instead too often anger and rage become expressed.[2] With a heavy heart I am aware that there can be abuse against women in relationships and in marriages. Tragically this cycle often results from the lack of healthy male figures in formative years or from fatherlessness.

I seek to allow God to use me to encourage men and honor them as God points out those whom He wants me to bless. Coincidently, even while writing this chapter the Lord led me to walk up to a man sitting in his car at a park. I gave him the "Prayers to Bless and Honor Men" handout and encouraged him with words the Holy Spirit gave me. I prayed for healing for him and blessed him. May he be awakened to the strength and dignity deposited inside him meant to bless those around him with God's plan for manhood.

⸙

---

[2] Remco Brommet, "A New Male Awakening," Intercessors for America, November 13, 2023, https://ifapray.org/blog/a-new-male-awakening/.

Sowing Seeds Through Honor

Lord our God, other lords besides you have ruled over us, but your name alone do we honor. Isaiah 26:13b

What is mankind that you are mindful of them, human beings that you care for them? You have made them a little lower than the angels and crowned them with glory and honor. Psalm 8:4–5

Whoever pursues righteousness and love finds life, prosperity and honor. Proverbs 21:21

Pride brings a person low, but the lowly in spirit gain honor. Proverbs 29:23

Be devoted to one another in love. Honor one another above yourselves. Romans 12:10

⚜

Man Walking on Sidewalk: Curse to Blessing – Kansas City, Missouri (August 2020)

I was on the sidewalk at a park waiting for my film producer Jerry to come for another outdoor shoot for the professional video of my "Jesus Rap." I saw a young man maybe in his thirties approaching and I felt the leading of the Holy Spirit to engage him in conversation to share the "Prayers for Men" handout that God gave me. Always awkward initially to interrupt a stranger, but from past experience I know it is almost always a blessing for the recipient and for me the giver. So, I said, "Excuse me, but God pointed you out to me and I wanted to share prayers to bless you. A few years ago, God told me to encourage, honor and bless men cuz they need it these days ... my name is Sally."

He looked surprised and said, "I can't believe it. You're the second person in an hour to speak to me about God. How'd you know? Truthfully, I think the men in our family are cursed. Wow, I can really use a blessing." (Oh Lord, thank you for helping me follow your leading.)

"Yeah, I would love to pray for you Kurt and agree with you that the power in Jesus' name will break every curse over you and the men in your family and instead bring blessing into your life."

I prayed. Kurt cried. The Holy Spirit led me in a powerful prayer for faith to grow, for Jesus to walk closely with Kurt, for the Holy Spirit to empower him and bring freedom. I prayed for protection and truths from the Prayer handout—that he'd have the faith of Abraham, the courage of Joshua, the wisdom of Solomon, the sovereign purposes of God fulfilled as in Joseph's life.

Providentially God had Jerry arrive late, so I even shared my rap with him which touched him. How amazing it is to have the Holy Spirit direct our lives to those who are hurting. Jesus came to set captives free and release prisoners from darkness (Isaiah 61:1).

Target Employee Blessed – Lee's Summit, Missouri (March 2017)

Well, it happened again. I'm going about my business at Target, saw a male employee who God pointed out to me, so I asked how his day was going. His answer led me to want to encourage him. I turned the conversation to faith and prayer and handed him one of my "Prayers to Honor Men" sheet. He said, "Wow, I need this. Thank you. My life is hard right now, and this encourages me." My heart was touched to bring a blessing to this man as I quietly thanked Jesus for letting me be His ambassador of hope.

Honor Prayers for Two Men – Kansas City, Missouri (January 15, 2020)

During the time that my husband Alan lived at the Veterans Home an hour away, I was waiting in the parking lot of the Kansas City Veterans Hospital to accompany Alan for a doctor's appointment. While waiting I struck up a conversation with Veer who was slowly walking across the parking lot. I found out that he had epilepsy and needed healing. I asked permission and prayed for him that Jesus would heal him. Then I felt led to give him the "Prayers to Honor Men" and blessed him, praying the specific sentence prayers from the sheet over him.

Immediately Veer gave me a big hug. Wow! Then I encouraged him in his spiritual life and he hugged me again as we said goodbye. Lord, You are so kind to bring such blessing to me even as I walked through great sorrow in seeing my husband suffer from his terminal illness. How grateful I am that You help me to "make the most of every opportunity" (Ephesians 5:16).

That same day, I went to the International House of Prayer to pray for a while, and I saw a mom and her son. I felt led to introduce myself and talked with them. I shared how God had spoken to me to honor men, so asked if I could pray for her son some prayers based on men of the Bible who are known for specific characteristics. She was thrilled that I would want to do this for her son Cohen. I prayed for him from the sheet and then gave it to him. He was touched and told me that he had been shot a year ago and has recovered and is in a Christian college and doing better. I agreed with his mom that God has a destiny for his life!

Grocery Store Suspicion to Smiles – Kansas City, Missouri (April 2022)

Often in my day-to-day life God puts it on my heart to go up to African-American men that in some small way I might be an instrument of racial healing. In the grocery store, walking down the aisle I saw two men shopping. They ignored me, but I felt that familiar leading to go up to them and share the "Prayers to Honor Men." I walked a few feet from my cart and said, "Excuse me." They looked up thinking I'm perturbed about something and gave me a suspicious look.

"Hey, I'm a person of faith and prayer, my husband was a military chaplain, and God told me to bless and honor men. Can I share these prayers with you that I wrote, and you could take them home and look at them later?" Well, they started to smile as I handed them the sheets and told them the prayers are based on men in the Bible and I hope they'll be encouraged. It isn't much, but it's my desire they'll be touched by Jesus and drawn into a closer walk with our Lord. Then I silently prayed God's blessing on them as I walked away.

Prayer

Father, You are a God of restoration. Please help men to receive a revelation of Your love for them and to be raised up as spiritual warriors for Your Kingdom purposes. Heal their hearts from wounds of fatherlessness and provide healthy mentors for them so they will walk in Your ways. Enable them to know who You created them to be and to be honored as they also extend honor. Use me in whatever way You lead to honor and show respect to the men and women in my life, all of whom bear the honor of being Your image bearers. Amen!

❦

5

Tears Matter to God

When Jesus saw her weeping … He was deeply moved in spirit and troubled. "Where have you laid him?" he asked.

"Come and see, Lord," they replied. Jesus wept.

John 11:33-35

Seasons of life vary, don't they? It's been a decade of tears in my life, but I think a new season of joy is opening before me. I have several young friends who are filled with joy as they await the birth of their first child. Other friends, especially those in the winter season of life, are walking in sorrow. For me, I'm in the third year of widowhood after walking with my dear husband through eight years of his terminal illness. So many tears. I'd have thought surely the supply would have run dry. My sweet Alan went to his heavenly home in December 2020 and then over the following two years I lost eight friends. Tears … tears … tears.

I think some of you know what I'm talking about or have been there. For some of you also, perhaps it is a season of tears? As Ecclesiastes says, "There is a time for everything … A time to weep and a time to laugh, a time to mourn and a time to dance" (Ecclesiastes 3:1,4).

Beyond our personal lives, our nation has been affected by greater isolation and loneliness, and less community, that is leading to more fragile emotional states in individuals. As a nation post pandemic, mental health experts have seen an increase of anxiety, depression and sadness with many struggling in daily life. There is also an enemy of our soul who wars against humanity and seeks to oppress and steal our joy and peace. So, for some, tears come too easily. But for followers of Christ, we have the Holy Spirit as our Helper and are able to rise above oppression and depression by looking to Jesus, to Scripture promises given to us, and to the hope of Heaven. Friends, be encouraged. Our faith is of greater worth than gold Scripture tells us and is proved genuine in trials and suffering (1 Peter 1:7). Our nation and loved ones look to us to stand strong in faith even when we go through seasons of tears.

I have experienced, in the midst of grieving and loss, surprising moments of supernatural joy and so can you. God's grace enables us to be strong because of His promises: He is with us, He is the Comforter, He has given believers the gift of His Holy Spirit to walk with us each day. We can choose to be grateful and offer God thanksgiving and worship for the blessings He gives. For me, I thank Him for the forty-six years of marriage I had to an incredible husband, for two wonderful children, wonderful grandkids, and a life rich with encountering wonderful people in Divine assignments. Yes, tears still fall some days, but I believe for all His children, there comes new seasons of more laughter and joy in daily life. Hold on to faith and hope if you're in a season of tears. Joy even comes surprisingly juxtaposed along with tears as happened to me while visiting my husband's grave at Arlington National Cemetery. Trust and surrender your heart to God whatever season you are in and put your hope in Him. He loves you and one day will wipe away all our tears.

Sowing Seeds When There Are Tears

Many verses in the Bible address how precious the tears of God's people are to Him. He designed our bodies to release powerful hormones when we cry, and Jesus Himself grieved as He walked on planet earth in a human body. Consider how these verses reflect God's heart about tears and grieving and how precious both are to God.

You keep track of all my sorrows. You have collected all my tears in your bottle. You have recorded each one in your book. Psalm 56:8

As he approached Jerusalem and saw the city, he wept over it and said, "If you, even you, had only known on this day what would bring you peace—but now it is hidden from your eyes." Luke 19:41-42

A woman who had lived a sinful life came ... knelt at His feet weeping, she began to wet His feet with her tears. Then she wiped them with her hair, kissed them and poured perfume on them. Luke 7:37-38

Those who sow in tears will reap with songs of joy. Those who go out weeping, carrying seed to sow, will return with songs of joy. Psalm 126:5-6

God himself will be with them and be their God. He will wipe every tear from their eyes. There will be no more death or mourning or crying or pain, for the old order of things has passed away. Revelation 21:3

❧✶❧

Tears Flowed at Grocery Store – Gardner, Massachusetts (November 2013)

As I was checking out in my hometown grocery store, the cashier Bonnie shared when I asked about her upcoming Thanksgiving, that it's a sad time because nineteen years ago her son drowned at a local pond. He had loved celebrating Thanksgiving. When she told us he was eighteen and had planned to go into the military, I began to cry and said, "Bonnie, we were there. My husband tried to save your son!"

We were visiting my hometown in Massachusetts while serving in the Navy. We were swimming at my sister's beach when we heard a call for help from a young man that his friend had gone under. Alan and my brother-in-law Bill tried to rescue the man's friend. They dove under numerous times desperately trying to find him but could not. It was very traumatic for all of us. For many years I had prayed for this woman. And today God had us meet in line as I was checking out.

She cried too, and I reached for her hand, and over tears, I told how we had lifted up many prayers for her for God's comfort in her grief. I shared that I had written a book about the suffering of Jesus who endured great trials and anguish while on earth. I went out to the car and brought one in for her. She was very touched that God had us meet and for the gift of my book. Tears matter to God.

God, please continue to bless Bonnie—how amazing that You brought us together. Touch Bonnie and those who are mourning with Your love and continued comfort.

のかどう

Lonely Man – Ocean Grove, New Jersey (August 20, 2018)

My husband and I were spending time walking the boardwalk at this quaint beach town and asked God perhaps to lead us to someone with whom we could share Christ. We saw a man sitting on a bench and felt the Holy Spirit prompt us to go up to him. We said hello and asked if we could pray for him about anything.

He said, "No, I'm OK," but then went on to tell us that he just broke up with girlfriend. I could tell he was in emotional pain. We spent time talking about God's love for him and His desire to be in a relationship with him. He was moved by our concern and compassion for him. I shared the Gospel and told him Jesus desires to extend grace as he is willing to humble himself, to ask for forgiveness and to seek to be born again from the Spirit. I shared my rap with him and then prayed. He was fighting back tears and was embarrassed and said he never cries. The Holy Spirit was touching him, but he said he wasn't ready to pray to receive Jesus.

Please pray for Carter. He was in a lot of emotional pain from rejection and had been on his own from age seventeen on. It was a beautiful time of sharing Jesus' compassion and seeing him moved to tears as God's presence came on him.

Coffee House – Final Rap Shoot – Kansas City (October 30, 2020)

We finished the final rap location shoot Saturday and took the volunteers out for dinner. A few of our group stopped at a store on the way so when we came in the three of us were seated. The waitress asked how our day was, and I blurted out how excited I was to have finished the final location shoot for a film production of my rap. She looked very surprised, and I started doing it for her but stopped partway. I told her it was a rap about God's love, and she looked intrigued. We talked a little bit, and then I felt led to share the second half of it. The Holy Spirit touched her, and she started to cry. She said it was so beautiful!

She was embarrassed and couldn't believe she was crying. It blessed me as confirmation from God that this has been His idea to make a professional video of the rap and see people touched by God's Spirit.

We prayed that God would work in Layla's life, and I encouraged her while she was serving us. She said she was blessed to have met us. The Lord was touching her, and I gave her a handout with Scripture prayers, and she thanked us. Thank you, Jesus, for this opportunity to bless her.

Gift Store – Frankenmuth, Michigan (September 10, 2021)

In a gift store, tears came as I walked by a section of military hats, and I saw the Navy hat that Alan always wore. I started crying and saw other items that triggered more tears. I told Jennifer to go out to let me stay there and cry in a private corner. After a few minutes I was still crying, and a woman my age walked by and looked with concern at me. I told her I was grieving the loss of my husband. She was very kind and let me share, telling me she understood as she was grieving the loss of her mom. I shared that Alan had been a Navy Chaplain and an amazing man of God. She was touched by that, and I could tell she was a believer. I mentioned Alan being the author of an amazing book given to him by spiritual dreams from God. She got excited and I also shared about my book on suffering that was a message I spoke to people with leprosy in India in 2012. She was very interested to hear about our books and wanted to look them up. I told her they were available on Amazon. I thanked her for her kindness letting me share and she said this was definitely meant to be and was blessed talking together.

Hawaiian Man at Historic Hotel – Boonville, Missouri (June 2022)

My friend Jane and I went on a weekend road trip to a quaint Missouri town Boonville (related to Daniel Boone) along the Lewis and Clark exploration trail. We had made reservations at the historic old Hotel Frederick. The desk clerk, Kai, was surprisingly from Hawaii (Oahu) where Alan and I were stationed for three years. I quickly connected with Kai, who was native Hawaiian, and had fun talking about Hawaii. On Sunday early morning, no one was in the lobby, we got onto spiritual conversation, and I was able to share my rap with him and he loved it. I shared with him about having a personal relationship with Jesus and encouraged him to find a local church. He really seemed hungry and blessed by our spiritual conversation. He was a lovely older man with a ponytail and earrings and a beautiful servant heart. Jesus touched him as he was moved to tears as I prayed for him and encouraged him in faith. Interesting that I was supposed to have been in Idaho but had canceled that trip—didn't feel strong enough to make it. So grateful to the Holy Spirit who led us to take a two-day trip and directed us to the Hotel Frederick. I was moved to tears to be a vessel of Jesus' love and grace. Kai and I hugged as Jane and I checked out. It was a very powerful Divine assignment. Thank you, Jesus. Please continue to draw Kai to yourself and bring him to a church for fellowship.

Airbnb Host Youth Pastor – O'Fallon, Missouri (May 2023)

The kindness of God was shown to me on Alan's birthday bringing me a special blessing. I felt led on my way back from Kentucky to stay in an Airbnb—although I had considered a Holiday Inn. When I arrived I quickly discovered the hosts were Christians—the husband a youth pastor. I had wonderful fellowship with Lisa as I got settled into my room. When I woke in the morning, I felt led to ask the Lord for a word of encouragement for Blake and I proceeded to write it down.

After breakfast I went upstairs and met Blake. Jesus touched him as I shared that the Lord gave me a Word to encourage him. As I read it to him, he was moved to tears. I prayed for him, and he was blessed and encouraged by what the Lord gave me. He thanked me for taking the time to do this. He and his wife also prayed for me.

A kiss from God because it was Alan's birthday, and I felt sad that I was driving four hours home and had no plans for the day. Usually, it helps to be with close friends to remember Alan on a day like today. But immediately in the morning I was blessed to feel that I was carrying on Alan's legacy of compassion and love, desiring to be a blessing to those around me. The Lord enabled me to do as Alan would have done—to bless this young couple and pray for them. They thanked me for stopping and being a blessing to them in my overnight stay at their Airbnb. I love how the Holy Spirit continues to give me boldness to be the light of Jesus—loving the people God puts in my path each day. Thank you, Father God. Thank you, Jesus. Thank you, Holy Spirit, for bringing me joy on this day.

❦

Prayer

Oh Jesus, Divine Comforter, You know what it's like to grieve. You were on Earth as a Man of Sorrows familiar with suffering (Isaiah 53:3). In Your time on Earth, You felt people's pain and You wept when Your friend Lazarus died. Thank You for the words You spoke to Your followers as the time drew near that on the cross You would give Your life to redeem mankind: "Do not let your hearts be troubled, do not be afraid. Trust in God trust also in me" (John 14:1). Tears are precious to You, Lord. You collect them in a bottle as David wrote (Psalm 56:8). May I find hope in Your promise that "Weeping may remain for a night, but joy comes in the morning" (Psalm 30:5). Give me Your heart to see and care for those around me who may be grieving. Amen.

6

Mishaps, Interruptions, and Frustrations
Jehovah Sneaky at Work

And we know that in all things God works for the good of those who love Him who have been called according to His purpose.

Romans 8:28

C an a sermon change a life? In 2008 I heard a Korean missionary share her God-given principle of seeing all that comes into her daily life as Divine setups allowing her to be the light of Christ. Whether in line at a store, in a taxi, on an airplane, or experiencing unexpected inconveniences, she uses every opportunity to share God's love and truth to those around her. The sermon really impacted me as I had been living my life to serve God by doing some weekly ministry, but day to day I had my own agenda and would be easily frustrated with interruptions or delays to accomplishing things on my daily to-do list.

I reflected on that sermon for many weeks and God had me look at it even deeper to see mishaps, interruptions, inconveniences, and frustrations as God-ordained for a greater purpose. Think about it with me. Really our lives are not our own as followers of Christ. Aren't we to surrender everything to Him—even our daily agenda? And can you see how life can become more of an adventure and more interesting to live this way? So, along with this new mission, I decided that I had a new name for God—Jehovah Sneaky: for the God who has a plan and purpose in what He allows in our life of faith even in the trying, irritating, difficult things. Perhaps Solomon who wrote the Proverbs had it right, "Many are the plans in a man's heart, but it is the Lord's purpose that prevails." Proverbs 19:21

As Christians we grow in the awareness that God can redeem the trials and hardships that come to us. An illustration of this is found in Acts 27-28 when the Apostle Paul is being sent to Rome to stand before Caesar with the charges brought against him. While sailing to Rome guarded by soldiers, they encounter a terrible storm and face great danger. An angel appears to Paul, revealing that they will encounter a shipwreck but will make it safely to shore. They find themselves on the island of Malta where the islanders show kindness to them. Paul is brought before the chief official of the island whose father is sick in bed suffering from fever. Paul prays for him, and he is healed. The rest of the sick on the island are brought to him and they also are healed. The name of the Lord was glorified in this mishap that happened to Paul, and I believe many were brought to faith in Jesus Christ on Malta.

A powerful Old Testament illustration is given in the story of Joseph (Genesis 39-50) whose brothers were jealous of him and sold him into slavery. However, God prospered Joseph over the many years of slavery he spent in Egypt as he sought to honor God. He was even wrongly imprisoned, but the Lord was with him and honored him while in prison. Joseph was known to interpret dreams and through a God-ordained occurrence he was brought before Pharaoh, the ruler of Egypt, and spoke a correct interpretation about a great famine that was to come to that region of the world. Pharaoh elevated Joseph to be the prime minister and after a period of time, his own brothers came before him asking for grain. Joseph battled to be able to forgive them, and because he looked so different, he was not known to them. Eventually he revealed himself to his brothers and his position enabled the Jewish nation to go down to Egypt and be provided for during the famine. Though his brothers feared what Joseph might do to them, he declared to them, "You intended to harm me, but God intended it for good to accomplish what is now being done for the saving of many lives" (Genesis 50:20). God's purposes played out in Jewish history in allowing this interruption, serious inconvenience, and bitter trial in Joseph's life.

Reflect on your life and what God may have allowed as mishaps, inconveniences, frustrations—small and large—for a greater good? Our life of faith can be empowered when we trust that He knows what He is doing in these situations. Again consider the acrostic for WITNESSES: Whatever Inconveniences/Interruptions to Normal Everyday Schedule Surrender Everything to the Spirit (who empowers us).

Sowing Seeds from the Mishaps of Life

So we are convinced that every detail of our lives is continually woven together for good, for we are his lovers who have been called to fulfill his designed purpose. Romans 8:28 (TPT)

Be very careful then how you live, not as unwise but wise, making the most of every opportunity." Ephesians 5:15-16

Now I want you to know, brothers and sisters, that what has happened to me has actually served to advance the Gospel. Philippians 1:12

Be joyful always; pray continually; give thanks and all circumstances, for this is the will of God for you in Christ Jesus. 1 Thessalonians 5:16-18

For my thoughts are not your thoughts, and your ways are not my ways, declares the Lord. For as Heaven is higher than the Earth so my ways are higher than your ways and my thoughts than your thoughts. Isaiah 5:8-9

∾⟨⟩∾

ER Visit – Spaced Out at Computer – Ft. Belvoir, Virginia (May 2012)

One morning Alan and I had the privilege to pray with four people at Ft. Belvoir Medical Center—a doctor, a nurse, a corpsman, and a patient. Alan didn't like how God got us there though.

I zoned out for an hour around 7 am while sitting at the computer. I was unresponsive to Alan—he noticed me staring off into space. He talked to me, and I didn't answer. Quite concerned, he brought me over to the sofa. I felt like I was in a daydream seeing his face in front of mine, talking, telling me he's calling 911, etc. But I had no thoughts; I don't even remember being brought into the ambulance but faintly heard a siren. I was taken to the ER at the army base and checked out thoroughly.

After an hour I started to talk. They did a CT scan—the results came back normal. A neurologist checked me out and was uncertain what had happened. She said I wasn't presenting as a TIA (mild stroke). Labs came back OK. God had Divine setups for prayer ministry though. My brain returned to functioning after a while and my mind decided prayer would be good, so we started looking for medical people to pray for. We prayed for comfort for Dr. Gill's family in the death of his grandmother; prayed for a husband for Jennifer, my nurse; and then prayed for wisdom and renewed commitment for Daniel, a corpsman, who wasn't walking close to the Lord, but whose mother named him Daniel from the Bible.

Finally, after discharge, I sat in the waiting area by Teresa as I waited for Alan to get the car. She really needed prayer as she was in chronic pain from three car accidents, had a sinus infection, fibromyalgia and just moved from Hawaii. She readily accepted my prayer for Jesus the Healer to touch her body with His Divine power, to overcome every pain, every attack of the enemy, to comfort and restore her. I invited her to our home Bible study, gave her my contact info, told her please come and we'll continue to believe for complete healing from God.

God had His plans and purposes at the hospital and as things turned around, we were glad to sow seeds of love and compassion to those we encountered at Ft. Belvoir Medical Center.

Bank of America in Red – Springfield, Virginia (August 2012)

Donations had slowed down for our non-profit Dunamis International Ministries—not sure why. We were concerned, as little money was coming in. I didn't know the exact amount in our account at Bank of America, but I wrote our monthly support check to India anyway supporting the Light Children's Home in Rajamundary. Later, looking at our monthly statement, I saw we had gone under by $600. I quickly looked at the checks we had received and went to make a deposit that day. It was late afternoon, and the outside window was closed, so I went inside to make a deposit.

No customers were in the bank at that time. I went up to the teller—a young man named Luke—to make the deposit. He seemed friendly and I shared with him about our ministry in India and about my book on God's redemptive purposes for suffering. I shared that my husband worked for Rev. Barry Black, the Chaplain of the US Senate and told him how God's Word had saved Chaplain Black's life from making a wrong decision that could have led to imprisonment.

Luke seemed very interested and told me he used to read the Bible regularly but had gotten away from the habit. I told him how important God's Word was for keeping us on the right path and helping us know God's will for our lives. I spoke encouragement into his life, and he was very open and appreciative.

Interesting that I would not have gone into the bank if we had not gone under with our account balance. I always use the outdoor window and realized God allows all sorts of inconveniences to get us to places where we can share our faith and be His witness.

Alan Diagnosed with Terminal Disease – Lee's Summit, Missouri (October 2016)

Sometimes the mishaps and interruptions of life bring incredibly challenging changes to lives of individuals. This was the case with my husband who after an MRI was told he was facing a degenerative brain disease and our future dreams of itinerant ministry came to a sudden halt. I decided to share briefly in this chapter as it seemed to fit in, though in a much more serious way than the other anecdotes I share.

Only by the grace of God did we receive this news knowing that we were going to be presented with different ministry opportunities than we thought. Alan had retired from the Navy in 2003 after twenty-three years serving as a military Chaplain. He had the privilege to then work at the US Senate for his former boss, Chaplain Barry Black. He served nine years there and showed signs of what I thought was burnout from too many years of high-level responsibility. We had hoped that after a season of rest, Alan would be refreshed, and we would travel the country in itinerant ministry.

Our ministry developed instead into praying for, listening to, and showing the love of Jesus for people at doctor's offices, in waiting rooms, hallways, and at the Kansas City Veterans Hospital and Veteran's Home. It was a very hard eight years, but we remembered the Scripture to *"make the most of every opportunity"* (Ephesians 5:16). So, we sought to be faithful to the Lord and allow Him to still live His life through us. God walked faithfully with us through those years, the Holy Spirit gave us strength, and Jesus' grace poured out to sustain us. Alan resided for a year at the local Veterans home where weekly I would bring my guitar and play hymns and have a short worship service for the veterans and their wives. Alan went home to Jesus December 2020 and received the words given to a true servant of God, *"Well done good and faithful servant."*

Lost Guitar Capo Brings Opportunity to Witness – Leawood, Kansas (April 2022)

"Why can't I find my guitar capo?" So frustrated. I don't lose things too often, but for several weeks I kept looking for my lost capo—a device used to change the key on the guitar. After a month, it dawned on me, "Oh Lord, is this a setup to give me a chance to be Your witness to someone at The Guitar Center store?"

It was. A young man was at the counter and showed me where the capos were located and left me there to decide which one I wanted. I made my choice and walked up to the counter to make my purchase. As the store had just opened there were not many customers, so after he took my payment, we started talking about music and guitars. The Holy Spirit enabled me to get on spiritual conversation and Eric was open to talking about faith. I told him my background—lost with no interest in the church as a young person, but after a few years of searching for meaning and purpose, I turned back to Jesus and church. He became real to me, I told Eric, and a deep emptiness was filled by the presence of God in my life.

I could tell he was receiving the words and truth I shared, and I laughed and told him, maybe my capo was lost for a purpose, so I could come in and encourage him to look to Jesus. He agreed and also received a Scripture handout and thanked me for sharing. An inconvenience turned into a blessing and chance to sow seeds into this young man's life.

❧

God Laughed – Keys Locked in Van – Overland Park, Kansas (March 8, 2022)

Oh no! I locked my keys in my van at my apartment complex. I had pulled over by the office to run in and get my mail. I came back out and couldn't find my van key. Ugh! My insurance company was called for roadside assistance to get into my van. I was told the wait could be sixty minutes. Meanwhile I thought, "Oh, maybe a Divine assignment?" I had the handout "Prayers for Men" that I give out regularly and one of Alan's books with me.

Elliott came in two minutes. He was a very nice young man, and he quickly unlocked my van for me. Before he left, I shared the prayers for men that I love to give out and encouraged him spiritually. I asked if he was a person of faith, and he said he was. I told him how God told me to honor men and commend them. Also, I felt called in a small way to be an instrument of racial healing—showing love to all my brothers and sisters. He seemed touched.

When asked if he was a reader, he said he was. So, I offered him Alan's book, and he told me he looked forward to looking at the book after work. I asked how I could pray for him—he said for strength, and to find a life partner. The Holy Spirit directed my prayer and we both were almost moved to tears. Jesus touched us both. He held up the book and said this was better than any tip. As Elliott drove away, he told me our meeting was meant to be, that he was blessed, and that he'd be in touch.

So, I got in my van as he drove off, reached in my purse for my key. No key! I looked on the floor, looked on the ground under my van, and asked at the office if anyone had turned in a key. Where was my key?

Then I remembered that the coat I was wearing had two side pockets—one with a flap and also a hidden side pocket. "No way God—don't tell me the key was never locked in my van but had been in the hidden pocket all the time." I reached in and there was my van key! OK God, you set this up for Elliott and me to meet, to talk and pray . . . a definite Divine assignment. God, I think You enjoyed the humor in this and had a good laugh. Well, You are an awesome God—Jehovah Sneaky!

Prayer

Father, please help me to surrender my life to You even when mishaps, interruptions, and inconveniences affect my daily plans. Holy Spirit, rule over my days, my hours, my schedule. I want to trust You God and allow You to live Your life through me. Help me to make the most of every opportunity that You give me to be Your witness. Give me boldness to share my faith and encourage others to look to You. Remind me to give thanks in all circumstances and to know that All things can work together for Your purposes—even really hard things. Take away self-centeredness so that I will find true joy in living a Christ-centered life. Amen!

7

Divine Synchronicity

Lord, I know that people's lives are not their own;
it is not for them to direct their steps.

Jeremiah 10:23

Synchronicity—an amazing word I've come to welcome in my life as a seed sower. I want to introduce this word to you in a new way perhaps, that will help to understand the stories in this chapter. This was not a word in my vocabulary until a few years ago when I was sharing with a friend how God sometimes orchestrates Divine assignments for me in unusual ways. When he explained those are probably moments of synchronicity and shared the meaning, I said, "Yup, that's it." A good explanation is a meaningful coincidence of two or more events. Additionally, it might be seen as a coincidence that has a profound effect on our life of faith—or an occurrence in life where something other than the probability of chance is involved. It is a term first coined by psychologist Carl Jung, and though different fields and people use the term in various ways, I am baptizing it by celebrating Gospel synchronicity.

An Old Testament example of synchronicity is found in the story of Esther. The Jews are in exile in Persia where the ruling king has vanquished his queen for a serious misdeed. A search is made for the beautiful young virgins of the land, and they are brought into the palace to be prepared to come before the king to make his choice of a new queen. Esther, whose Jewish name is Hadassah, is also taken, but is told by her uncle who raised her to keep secret that she is a Jew. In God's sovereign plan for his people Esther is chosen as the new Queen. She is in a place to have influence when an enemy of the Jews, the chief official Haman, devises a plot to destroy them because of his hatred against Esther's uncle Mordecai. A decree is made of a day of destruction. Mordecai, fasting and weeping for his people, sends an urgent message to Esther to go to the king to beg for mercy for her people.

He declares, "Who knows but that you have come to this royal position for such a time as this?" It is a powerful moment of synchronicity for the Jewish people to have Esther their queen able to find favor with the king. Another decree is sent out, allowing the Jews to defend themselves when the day of their destruction comes. God has brought together an unlikely orchestration of a young Jewish woman raised up to be queen of a pagan people in order that God's chosen people would be spared.

A New Testament example of synchronicity is found in Jesus' ministry to a thirsty Samaritan woman when He offers her the gift of living water. He encounters her at a well in the heat of midday. Jews hated Samaritans, who were a mixed race of Jews and Gentiles, and normally would not even travel through Samaria. Jesus, however, led His disciples through this region on their way to Galilee. A Divine setup is about to happen.

Jesus, tired from the journey, sits down by the well; He is alone as He has sent His disciples on ahead to buy food. A thirsty woman comes to the well and is shocked that Jesus speaks with her—Jewish rabbis would never do this. In a moment of synchronicity, the source of Living Water encounters a thirsty woman who hears of the free gift of eternal life. Jesus speaks to her in love, truth and compassion. Her soul thirst is satisfied, she puts her faith in the Messiah, and her life is forever changed.

Our omnipotent God also desires to raise us up as people of faith to touch our world. "For we are God's workmanship created in Christ Jesus to do good works which God prepared in advance for us to do" (Ephesians 2:10). The following stories I believe are setups of Divine synchronicity—meaningful coincidences of time and place for accomplishing God's Kingdom purposes.

Sowing Seeds Through Synchronicity

I will instruct you and teach you in the way you should go; I will counsel you with my loving eye on you. Psalm 32:8

And who knows but that you have come to your royal position for such a time as this? Esther 4:14

God, who went ahead of you on your journey, in fire by night and in a cloud by day, to search out places for you to camp and to show you the way you should go. Deuteronomy 1:33

In Him we were also chosen, having been predestined according to the plan of Him who works out everything in conformity with the purpose of His will. Ephesians 1:11

Show me the way I should go, for to You I entrust my life. Psalm 143:8b

eↄↄↄↄↄ

Seatmate on Airplane – Colorado Springs, Colorado (May 10, 2010)

"We're gonna miss our flight!" Alan and I had spoken at a conference in Colorado Springs, were exhausted and went to sleep without checking our email. We missed seeing the email notifying us that our flight had been moved to an earlier time. We woke the next morning and became aware we were not going to be able to make our flight. Immediately we called the airline who arranged for us to take a flight out of Denver. So, we scrambled to get on the road and drive the two hours to Denver to catch that flight. Thankfully we made it, and then Divine synchronicity happened.

Our seatmate on the plane shared how she also had missed her flight and so wasn't supposed to be on that plane either: a Divine setup. Carly was a bank executive who was ready for a career change. We engaged in casual conversation and then shared our faith in Jesus Christ and testimony of how God is able to direct our lives. Carly was very open to hearing of the personal relationship we had with Christ. We also told her we planned to go on a mission trip in November to India to visit an orphanage. She stated, "I'd like to go with you. Yes, I'm going with you."

She did. A complete stranger one moment—who through Divine synchronicity had her life dramatically changed. She joined us on our ten-day trip to India, but Carly stayed three months. She grew into a strong woman of God, and to this day she is a beautiful, devoted follower of Christ.

Veteran with PTSD at Park – Houston, Texas (September 28, 2014)

Sightseeing north of Houston, Alan and I stopped at a park for lunch where a young man was playing frisbee with his dog. We engaged him in conversation, found out he was a firefighter and had been on missions in Iraq while in the Army. Alan shared that he had been in combat in Desert Storm as a Navy chaplain and how important it is to know God and hear God speak. He told Douglas that during combat he heard God's voice: "Shine your flashlight down ahead of your vehicle," discovering he was in a minefield. This saved Alan's convoy from death or injury.   Douglas shared he had been very religious as a teenager and had been on mission trips. But he had seen some terrible things during his assignment, he had teammates killed, and had received injuries, and now God seemed very distant. He didn't see how God could allow such terrible tragic deaths and suffering.

We told him of our books—Alan's book on destiny and mine on suffering—and that God had a purpose in having saved his life. I explained that the trials and painful things we encounter in life can have a redemptive purpose as we place them in God's hands. We shared that we don't understand the mystery of suffering and why bad things happen, but that we know Jesus Himself was a man of suffering. We can experience the God of comfort walking with us through our pain and trials.

God definitely set this up in the way He led us to this particular park at just the time Douglas was there. We believe God wanted us to pray for Douglas, to invite him back to a relationship with God and bring healing from the PTSD. Lord, bless Douglas and others struggling with PTSD—bring healing, comfort, and the knowledge of Christ's love.

Appalachia Hikers – Boiling Springs, Pennsylvania (October 10, 2014)

God is amazing! After our fourth day driving nine to ten hours to get home to Massachusetts from Colorado, we stopped at Boiling Springs, Pennsylvania to stay overnight with a precious ministry couple, Pastor Jesse and Kay Owens (our spiritual parents). They live near the Appalachian trail, and we were meeting them at a restaurant right off the trail. Because lunch had been delayed, to our frustration, we were an hour later than we expected to be arriving in Boiling Springs.

As we waited for the Owens, we saw a young couple with huge backpacks looking at the restaurant menu posted outside the front door. Immediately, I felt led to go up to ask where they were from and felt the Lord wanted us to pay for their meal, as the restaurant is a bit pricey. I walked up, engaged them in conversation and shared that God told us to treat them to dinner and they were blown away. Well, I was blown away as they shared that they were missionaries with YWAM (a Christian ministry) and were hiking the trail to minister to fellow hikers and didn't know if they had funds for dinner. We love being God's instruments of blessing and smiled that God orchestrated our ten-hour drive so we arrived just when they were walking up to the restaurant.

We heard about their adventures—they had been hiking since April and God had placed many in their path with whom they shared faith and prayed. We heard an amazing story of churches in Damascus, Virginia near the Appalachian Trail where Christians meet hikers to offer meals, do laundry for them, and even wash and massage their feet! They were told that seventy-two hikers had accepted Christ from this humble service offered to tired, sore hikers in simple acts of being Christ to those in need. They told us that they hope to go to China to be missionaries in the near future—what a wonderful young couple.

Consider what simple acts of service and the seeds that can be sown when in our communities we can be the hands and feet and eyes and ears of Jesus to those in need?

Ivy, My Seatmate – Enroute to Kansas City from Houston, Texas (January 8, 2019)

Better late than early sometimes for fulfilling God's assignments. I couldn't check in on time with Southwest as I was in the air flying yesterday. So, I was late checking in for my January 3rd flight. "Oh well," I thought. Because of this, I was in the B40 position for Southwest for boarding, putting me at the end of the boarding line with seats available in the back of the plane. As I walked down the aisle, I felt led to sit by a young woman. Yup, a God assignment.

Ivy was a college student at Marshall College in West Virginia. Her parents were very religious, but she was not so much. She was pursuing nursing and wanted to travel maybe with Doctors Without Borders to difficult places to care for the poor, the hurting, and needy. I commended her for this.

I was able to share my testimony and the importance of faith. I spoke my rap, which she really liked. I asked about her life—but she got teary when I asked about siblings. She didn't say what had happened, but I prayed for her and shared about suffering. Life is hard sometimes, but comfort comes to us through Christ. He walks with us in hard times. She fought back tears as I encouraged her and shared Jesus' compassion.

I also spoke about the Holy Spirit and told her my prayer—"Use me, fill me, possess me Holy Spirit, make me like Jesus." I told her about the gifts of God's Spirit that still operate through the lives of believers like in the book of Acts and how exciting it is to witness miracles and signs and wonders flowing through Christ followers. I told her again how proud God is of her desiring to live a life of service. I shared that God would direct her as she followed Him.

It was a beautiful time with Ivy … she was very touched by Jesus. Toward the end of the flight, she mentioned again how her parents are very religious, but she needed something to motivate or point her in the right direction. God used me to do that. She was very sweet, and we exchanged contact info to connect sometime in future. I told her to call or contact me if she needed to talk or pray. God's timing is perfect.

❧

Surprised at Evangel Church – Kansas City, Missouri (May 2021)

One Sunday the Holy Spirit led me to visit Evangel Church and during singing I was drawn to a woman nearby with a worship posture like I sometimes take— a hand on her heart and another hand lifted up. I kept looking at her and felt I was supposed to talk to her after the service. After worship I moved over to sit behind her and then waited for the end of the service.

I was impressed to tell her that she's the daughter of God's heart, that He was proud of her and that she was dear to him. We connected in conversation, and I asked if she's a member there. God's synchronicity came into play as she shared.

She was visiting that day—I was visiting that day. She was a pastor's wife—I was a pastor's wife. Her husband died last year—my husband died last year. Hmm ... What's up, God?

Well, we both were quite surprised. I asked if she had time for lunch. She did, so we picked up lunch and visited at my house. Three hours later we were bonded as friends and determined we would stay in touch. Incredible how the Holy Spirit impressed on me so strongly to visit Evangel Church. Thank You, Holy Spirit. I love you and appreciate your direction and leadership in life.

಄಄ఌ಄ఌ

Prayer

Father, how wonderful are Your plans for our lives. Open my eyes to see how You orchestrate situations in my life for Your plans. Help me trust You and believe that Your higher purposes will be fulfilled as we live our lives seeking to follow Your guidance. By Your Spirit may I see things afresh even to Your working by Divine synchronicity. Help me not to take unexpected occurrences in life for granted, but to believe and have faith that You know what You are doing. In Jesus' name. Amen.

8

My Feet Made Me Do It

How beautiful are the feet of those who bring good news.

Romans 10:15

I love that God has given us in our earthly journey some wonderful gifts including the gift of humor. Some of the experiences and opportunities in the life of faith come in a funny way. For example, I sometimes experience my feet having a mind of their own. Seriously. They just take over in either leading me where I wasn't planning to go or refusing to move from where I am standing.

Concerning "feet" we read in Scripture that one piece of our spiritual armor is having our feet fitted with the Gospel of peace (Ephesians 6:15). Our feet can lead us near and far—near into our neighborhoods—far onto a mission field: bringing us to individuals who need to hear about the Prince of Peace. Our Lord Jesus, who brings peace into our souls, makes us His ambassadors to help others receive reconciliation with Father God.

Jesus moved according to the will of the Father during His time on Earth. "For I have come down from heaven not to do my will but to do the will of him who sent me" (John 6:38). As He began His ministry, He discerned the will of God and called those who were to become His disciples. We might see humor in the moment when Jesus stopped by a tax collector's booth. He slowed down as His feet turned and took Him to Levi. "'Come and follow me,' Jesus said" (Mark 2:13-14).

Scripture doesn't give us what other dialogue may have followed among Jesus' followers, but remembering that the Jews hated tax collectors who served the Romans and oppressed their own people, I think perhaps it may have sounded like this.

"What are you doing Jesus? Why are you stopping?"

"Don't you see this man is a tax collector."

"Surely, Lord, you're making a mistake."

"Come on, let's move our feet and keep walking ... Jesus, you can't be serious."

But Jesus was serious. He called Levi the tax collector, who is more commonly known as Matthew, and Matthew not only followed Jesus as a disciple but also wrote the book of Matthew bearing his name.

In a second story concerning a tax collector in Luke 19:1-10 we read of Jesus entering Jericho intending to pass through. Along the way Jesus came to a spot where His feet stopped, undoubtedly under the leadership of the Spirit. Looking up into a Sycamore tree Jesus saw Zacchaeus who, being a short man, had climbed the tree for a better view of Jesus.

"Zacchaeus come down, I will stay at your house today." Convicted by being in the presence of the Son of God, Zacchaeus repented of greed and selfishness and received salvation. The story concludes with these beautiful words, "For the Son of Man came to seek and save what was lost" (Luke 19:10).

I believe if we're discerning like Jesus, our feet also will either bring us to the one who is lost or stay rooted until we speak life-giving words, boldly by the Spirit sharing the Gospel of Peace.

Sowing Seeds Through God-Directed Steps

How beautiful upon the mountains are the feet of him who brings good news. Isaiah 52:7

In his heart man plans his course, but the Lord determines his steps. Proverbs 16:9

I know, O Lord, that a man's life is not his own; it is not for man to direct his steps. Jeremiah 10:23

Trust in the Lord with all your heart and lean not on your own understanding; in all your ways acknowledge Him and He will direct your paths. Proverbs 3:5-6

The steps of a good man are ordered by the Lord, and He delights in his way. Psalm 37:23

But I say, walk by the Spirit, and you will not gratify the desires of the flesh ... If we live by the Spirit, let us also keep in step with the Spirit. Galatians 5:16, 25

Because of the tender mercy of our God, by which the rising sun will come to us from heaven to shine on those living in darkness and in the shadow of death, to guide our feet into the path of peace. Luke 1:78-79

RV Park and Campground – St Charles, Louisiana (April 10, 2013)

While checking out of a Louisiana campground ready to go to a new location in our RV, Alan and I wondered whether there was an opening to talk of spiritual things with the office manager. I was ready to get on the road, but the Spirit had my feet planted in place and didn't let me move. So, I asked my favorite question to Sarah, "Is there anything I can pray with you about in your life?"

She smiled, hesitated, and mentioned "strength" and shared how she didn't often bother God about things but mostly tried to be thankful. Alan and I both shared how that attitude pleased God, but that He also cares about things that concern us.

I mentioned the abundant life in Christ—how through a relationship with Jesus we can have inner peace, love, and joy—and how Jesus reconciled us to the Father, showing us how to live. She smiled then and shared how there was a man who had lived in the park and was quite hateful. He lived alone with three dogs and recently was diagnosed with bad cancer all through his body. Sarah was troubled about the state of his soul and asked a Christian lady in the park to go visit him when he was put on hospice care.

The lady went several times to speak to him about faith in Christ and eternity and finally came back one day and told Sarah, "He did it." He made his peace with God and the next day the Lord took him home. I had tears in my eyes and felt God's presence as Sarah related the story of this man's salvation in his final days. I asked if I could pray for Sarah before we left and asked God's blessing on her work and her life. She thanked us and said, "You made my day!" I hadn't really wanted to stay and talk, but the ole' feet wouldn't let me move. Thanks feet, you made our day!

Michael at Picnic Area – Shawnee Mission Park, Kansas (May 17, 2020)

I was happily anticipating meeting my friends Abigail and Andrew and their five boys outdoors during the covid pandemic. Arriving at a nearby picnic area, I parked my car, walked through the pavilion and saw Abigail waiting to greet me. But the Holy Spirit stopped me in my tracks as I looked to my left and saw a young man reading a book. Immediately words came out. "Is that a good book you're reading?"

He answered that he was reading The Color Purple. I don't know what I said next, but my feet brought me over to him. I shared that I'm a person of faith and asked if he was. He said yes. Then I shared that God had put on my heart to honor men by writing prayers based on men in the Bible. I told him I didn't have any on me, though I usually carry them to give out. But asked if I could bless him today and pray over him. He said, "Sure, and today is my birthday!"

"Wow," I said, "and you're here enjoying the park?" He said he would see family later. So, I blessed him with the faith of Abraham, the courage of Joshua, the wisdom of Solomon, the boldness of Paul, and the deep love that John had with Jesus. I gave him another Bible handout I had on me called "Our Life in Christ," which had my contact info so he could email me, and I'd send him the "Prayers to Honor Men."

Holy Spirit, you are so amazing. You stopped my feet to engage this young man and pray Your blessing on his birthday. Draw him deeper into a relationship with you Jesus!

❧

Powerful Encounter with My Neighbor – Kansas City, Missouri (August 10, 2021)

I had lived a year next door to two men, Jonathan and Ben, but hardly ever saw them to talk. They stayed to themselves. I had one conversation with Ben prior to covid, finding out that he performed in a circus with a unique talent. For a year I had been praying for them—for God's love to touch them, for light overcoming darkness and for God's blessings upon their lives.

So, though I was tired, and it was my last day in the house—the next day it was going on the market—I saw Ben outside and called out to him and he walked over. (God directed his feet to bring him to me.) Incredibly, we had a long talk! I told him I was praying for nice new neighbors for them.

"Oh, you're moving," he responded. I shared that though we hadn't spoken much the past year, I had been praying for them both. I told him since my husband Alan's recent passing it had been a difficult last year. I was hoping to travel and do ministry as God leads which brings me joy even in sorrow. I told him I had written a book on suffering and how God can redeem all we go through in life. I shared that I had experienced a difficult childhood and know life can be hard.

Ben answered, "Well, what you didn't know is I am like you. I lost my wife six years ago tragically and it's been a really hard six years." I was shocked and had no idea. Also, he too had a rough childhood with abuse. But he said the past few months the darkness had lifted and he was doing better. We were connecting at a deep level, and I realized God had heard my prayers even though I barely ever talked with them.

I asked if I could share my book with him and he got excited. I got him a copy of my book and he said, "Can I hug you?" He then told me how much he appreciated our talk.

We parted and I got into my car, moved to tears that though I felt like a failure in not being much of a witness the past year, God had used my prayers. And He gave me a last chance when Ben came outside at just the right moment and used his feet to bring him over to me. Two people on the same journey sharing deeply and looking to God for strength and grace. God, You are so good. Help Jonathan and Ben and all of our neighbors to know Your love and grow in faith.

Divine Setup in Spite of Hesitation – Leawood, Kansas (March 2022)

It was a cloudy morning, but I decided to go for a walk at Tomahawk Creek Trail. I felt a letdown after two days of ministry opportunities and there was fresh grief as I had dreamt about Alan. "God, I miss him so much." I allowed tears to come as I sat on a bench, looking out over the lake. When it started sprinkling, I went back to my car and sat there for a while. I had my prayer handouts but didn't have any conversations on the trail. I noticed a blue car next to me and was drawn to the young woman sitting eating her lunch. I wondered if I had the nerve to walk up to her window, wave to her and see if she would roll down her window and let me talk to her. I kept hesitating, changing my mind probably five times, but kept feeling I was supposed to go up to her car.

Finally, "What the heck—I'm going to do it." So, I walked over to her car and gave an awkward wave—she smiled and rolled down her window a few inches.

I said, "Hi, I noticed you sitting beside me. I'm a person of faith and just felt led to say hello and encourage you with these prayers that I wrote for women. I told her my husband was a military chaplain and that I love to bless people. I guess she assumed I was safe, so she rolled down her window the rest of the way. She looked like she was maybe in her late twenties. I introduced myself and she told me her name was Destiny. We chatted a little bit and I told her how God sometimes points out people for me to bless. I told her recently I became a widow, but have my spirit lifted when I meet and share my faith with others.

"My grandmother would like this prayer sheet," she said. "She owned a Christian bookstore in the area."

I abruptly interrupted and asked, "Ruth?"

She looked at me with amazement and said, "Yes!"

"Oh my gosh, she's my friend. She just came to my house for lunch.

She goes to my church—that's your grandmother?" We both laughed and couldn't believe this small world. We chatted a few more minutes, amazed at the connection.

I went home and called Ruth who picked up and laughed when I said, "Hi, it's Sally."

"Destiny already called me to tell me what happened." I told her how I hesitated five times, but the Holy Spirit prompted me to obey and go over to her car. She told me how she's praying for her granddaughter's faith to grow. She was blessed that I obeyed the Spirit.

So wonderful to be used by God and especially right after I had cried and had red eyes and red nose. Thank You, God, that we can be an instrument of Your grace and love.

⌒⌒⌒✶⌒⌒⌒

Firestone Mechanic Compassion Directed My Feet – Overland Park, Kansas (July 2023)

After a minor incident, I had to drop off my car at the garage to have some work done. After I parked, I started walking to the door and I saw a mechanic standing eating a donut before beginning a shift. It was one of those mornings I really didn't want to extrovert.

I wasn't feeling well so I didn't think I was going to say much, but I asked how he was doing, and he said OK. I asked if he worked a normal 8-5 day. He said yes, except he's getting off early to go to the doctor for some appendix problem.

Well, Jesus' heart of compassion activated in me. My feet turned without really wanting to and I walked closer to him. I decided that I would offer him the "Prayers for Men," and my feet continued to take me up to stand beside him.

I shared with him about God wanting me to bless and encourage men and handed him the prayer sheet. He smiled and thanked me. I asked if he was a person of faith, he said he was raised going to church, but not so much now. I gave a very quick testimony of my life and shared how Jesus is real and makes a difference in our lives and how wonderful to be able to have a relationship with Him. Then I asked if I could pray for him. When he agreed, I lifted up a prayer standing by the garage open doors. The Holy Spirit and my feet had collaborated so that I could represent Jesus' concern for this young man.

❧❀❧

Prayer

Holy Spirit, take control of my feet and direct them to where You would have me go. Help me see people as You see them, love people as You love them, and say to them what You would have me speak. I want to trust You fully with my daily agenda. I want to have boldness and give You control of my lips too as You direct my steps. Lord, I believe You will give me words to speak to those who are hurting or those who have their hearts being drawn to You. Help me obey Your Holy Spirit's prompting and experience adventures in my day-to-day life to make You known and bring You glory. I pray in Jesus' name. Amen.

❧❀❧

9

God's Compassion in His People

As a father has compassion on his children,
so the Lord has compassion on those who fear him.

Psalm 103:13

I walked past the airport employee but was impressed to do a U-turn and go back to her. She was standing on the side in the terminal, on break eating a snack. I had forty-five minutes until my boarding time and was on the lookout for who God wanted me to talk with during this time. I had a very strong impression about this lady, so I turned around and walked up to her. I said my normal intro of being a person of faith and prayer and told her that God had pointed her out to me. Then I asked if I could pray for her.

She grabbed my hands and said with deep emotion, "Yes please. My son died last week, and I would love prayer. I am trusting God to walk with me through this, but it's really hard." I was stunned and then remembered how strongly I felt the prompting to do the U-turn and come back to her. I told her my husband had died in December, and I was grieving too. We held hands, tears in our eyes, as we felt God's compassion for one another and prayed. Newly discovered sisters in

Christ, we hugged and felt God's love and presence in the midst of airport travelers walking past us. It was a holy moment connecting us to His heart for those in pain.

Jesus calls us to live as He lived in this world. We are indwelt by His Spirit connecting us with His heart that feels the pain of those who suffer. The Spirit Filled Bible offers this commentary on compassion:

> Christ likeness calls us to learn Jesus' heart of compassion, a depth of sensitivity that can be worked in us through the Holy Spirit, reconditioning our hearts to be able to sense the pain of human bondage and to weep with those who weep. (Romans 12:15). His compassion brought tears for the hardness of all hearts that were blinded by their sin and for the tragedy of all mankind's vulnerability to death. Love sees beyond the immediate and the personal, and compassionately relates to the lost, the hurting, the needy, the distressed.[3]

Compassion is to be moved so deeply you feel for others what they are experiencing. From the Hebrew word splanchna meaning bowels, which is the place from which the Hebrews thought emotions originated, compassion causes us to feel the deeper emotions enabling us to feel sympathy, affection, and pity for another.[4] There are times in my day-to-day life when God places someone in my path or points out an individual to me directing me to be the hands and heart of His compassion for those who suffer.

In India, in a Target parking lot, in the Houston Airport, at a beach, I've experienced compassion beyond my own ability to feel for another. It comes upon me from the loving heart of Father God creating an opportunity to connect that person with God's desire to bring comfort, healing or encouragement. Jesus evidenced this many times while he was on Earth. One that touches me deeply is when He encounters a widow whose only son died. Jesus enters a town, and a funeral procession is taking place. Luke shares what occurred. "When

---

[3] *New Spirit-Filled Life Bible.* Thomas Nelson, Inc., 2002, 1306.
[4] Ibid, 1306-1307.

the Lord saw her, He had compassion, His heart went out to her and he said, 'Don't cry.' Then he came and touched the open coffin and those who carried him stood still and he said, 'Young man, I say to you, arise.' So he who was dead sat up and began to speak, and Jesus presented him to his mother" Luke 7:13-15 (NKJV).

What opportunities might be presented to us in our daily life of faith when we could love as Jesus loves, speak as Jesus speaks, and care with hearts of compassion?

Sowing Seeds Through Compassion

"In a surge of anger, I hid my face from you for a moment, but with everlasting kindness I will have compassion on you," says the Lord your Redeemer. Isaiah 54:8

A man with leprosy came to him and begged him on his knees, "If you are willing, you can make me clean." Filled with compassion, Jesus reached out his hand and touched the man. "I am willing," he said. "Be clean!" Immediately the leprosy left him, and he was cured. Mark 1:40-41

Jesus went through all the towns and villages, teaching in their synagogues, proclaiming the good news of the kingdom and healing every disease and sickness. When he saw the crowds, he had compassion on them, because they were harassed and helpless, like sheep without a shepherd. Matthew 9:35-36

Praise be to the God and Father of our Lord Jesus Christ, the Father of compassion and the God of all comfort. 2 Corinthians 1:3

The Lord is gracious and compassionate, slow to anger and rich in love. The Lord is good to all; He has compassion on all He has made. Psalm 145:8-9

Therefore, as God's chosen people, holy and dearly loved, clothe yourselves with compassion, kindness, humility, gentleness and patience. Colossians 3:12

PhD Grocery Bagger – Colorado Springs, Colorado (October 3, 2014)

A bit of frustration came on us on the way to see the Air Force Academy in Colorado Springs. Alan and I had tried to find a place for lunch at two shopping areas—one had no parking, the other no decent restaurant. So, we went into the Commissary on base and got some sushi. Needing directions, Alan walked over to an older man who had brought groceries out for a customer.

We started to converse and then God showed up. We mentioned we were on a road trip and were ministers; he brightened and said he was in ministry also. Then he shared his struggles: he had a PhD, had taught at a university, was laid off, and couldn't find a job.

He said with a laugh, "I think I'm the only bagger here who has a PhD." We talked of trials and challenges in our lives. I shared my book on suffering with him, as he had said how much his wife was struggling with her mom having dementia. He was very grateful for the book. Then we prayed for him standing outside in the parking lot between cars and God touched him and he started to cry. We prayed for God's living water to refresh him, for God's presence to strengthen him, and for God's perfect will for his life. We were blessed to have sweet fellowship there in the parking lot. So, God had a reason we didn't find a parking spot earlier, as He wanted us to meet Henry and encourage him.

ᕁᕁᕁ

Erika Gas Station Attendant Grieving – Kansas City, Missouri (August 8, 2020)

Stopping for gas at a local station I filled up and wondered if God wanted me to talk to the attendant. She looked around thirty years old, tattooed all over, and she was talking on her phone. I hesitated. It was 7:00 a.m. I was the only customer. The Holy Spirit impressed on me to speak with her. I introduced myself and offered her the "Blessing Prayers for Women."

She said, "Yes, I'll read them. My sister died yesterday—she was thirty-five. It was a drug overdose… She has three boys … I'm having such a hard time." Jesus' compassion filled my heart. I asked if I could pray for her. Natalie started crying as I laid my hand on her shoulder and prayed for God's strength, comfort, and grace to be upon her. She told me she had to plan the funeral and was working to support herself. Everything felt so hard. I also prayed that God would be with those three boys—helping them to know His love and comfort and that He is Savior and friend. Compassionate Lord, walk with Natalie during the days ahead, lead her and wrap her in Your arms of love.

❧

Target Employee Encouraged – Lees Summit, Missouri (May 28, 2018)

I was shopping at Target. Ella, an employee I had met previously, helped me out to the car with my 24-pack water. Two months ago, I had met her when she assisted me with a heavy item. I had prayed for her in the parking lot and encouraged her. She had shared that she was a believer and appreciated prayer as her grandfather had recently died and her young cousin had cancer. I had been led by God to give her one of my books on suffering. She had been touched by my caring for her and in my praying for her.

So today I saw her again. She told me that she's in the middle of reading my book and recently went through a very hard crisis in her life. As we walked out to my car, she told me her ex-boyfriend committed suicide and she was devastated. Shaken by this tragedy, she remembered my book on suffering which I had given her and began reading it; it was blessing her. We had met in time so that she was able to come through this pain with God's help and with encouragement from the body of Christ.

She thanked me and said she's so grateful that God connected us. I started crying as I told her I'm struggling with my self-worth and how little I feel I do for God. Yet I was touched in return by her telling me she's reading my book and was blessed by my prayer and the time we spent together in the parking lot.

It is amazing how when I pray for the Holy Spirit to use me, allowing His compassion and love to pour through me to those who are hurting, He answers my prayer. My prayer the past few months is that God would release the power of His Spirit into my life to touch the world. As my husband used to say, often it happens one person at a time. But in doing that, we can make a difference in the world. Ella also said that her aunt is anxious to read my book when she's done with it. She told me too that her cousin we had prayed for who had cancer is doing better. Things are going better right now for her. So that was a blessing to hear. How kind of God to answer my prayer that my book would be a blessing to people. God, thank you for the privilege of sharing Your love and compassion, everywhere we go. I love You Jesus.

Ministry to Medical Staff – Lee's Summit, Missouri (February 18, 2021)

Once again I was having health issues and prayed, please use me to bless and encourage someone I meet. This time they scheduled me for an MRI and while there the two technicians received Scripture handouts and encouragement. They heard I rapped and said, "Let's hear it!" So right there in the office, they did. One tech came over and hugged me. That touched me that she was so blessed by the "Jesus Rap."

Then today, I went to the doctor and felt led to give her Alan's book, and she was encouraged. After the appointment, I went to the Lab and the technician Laura received prayer that Jesus would comfort and strengthen her as she recently became a widow too. She had tears as Jesus made His love real to her. She said she wanted to give me a hug but held back with covid concern. I'm so thankful the light of Jesus still shines forth. I prayed before going to the clinic, "Lord, use me to touch someone today and be a blessing." My heart was touched as Laura said that God used me to bless her. In His kindness God answered my prayer and allowed our paths to cross today.

ᐉᡩᔛᡃᢀᡅ

Man at the Beach – Templeton, Massachusetts (July 24, 2021)

While I was visiting my sister in Massachusetts, we went to a nearby lake for a swim. I noticed a man around forty sitting alone on a log reading. He had braces on his arm and leg—I felt compassion for him. I told my sister, Irene, that the Holy Spirit was leading me to go up to him. I walked over and introduced myself and told him that God has led me to bring encouragement to people spiritually with prayer handouts. I also shared my brief testimony. Greg said he was a believer but hadn't been to church for a while. I heard his story—he had a stroke, and had been quite depressed the first year. He couldn't talk very well and his right side was affected. Then peace came as he asked God to be with him. He received partial recovery and continued to trust God to be with him in this challenging season. We talked a long time about trials and suffering, and I prayed for him—for healing, strength, and God's grace to help him. I invited him to my sister's church nearby where I was invited to speak and share my raps.

The next day at my sister's church I was excited to see Greg in the congregation. God is so good. The Holy Spirit powerfully came through in the words presented. The congregation was blessed by the "Jesus Rap" and my message of living by God's WWW: Worship, the Word, and Witnessing. I hugged him after the service letting him know how happy I was to see him there. In the months ahead Greg continued to attend Hope Bible Church and got connected with the Body of Christ.

ᐉᡩᔛᡃᢀᡅ

Prayer

*God of compassion, make my heart break for what breaks Your heart.
Let me grow in compassion to feel the pain others feel and allow Your love to
pour through me to comfort, support, and lift up others in pain. In everyday
life let my eyes see as You see. Let me feel what others are feeling and speak
words that will allow them to know there is a loving God who cares deeply
for all that concerns them. Holy Spirit, lead me to the one who needs to know
someone cares—even a stranger who might become a friend as I seek to be
Your instrument to bring hope to this broken world. Amen!*

10

Uber Ministry:
On the Road with Jesus

*These commandments that I give you today are to be on
your hearts. Impress them on your children. Talk about them
when you sit at home and when you walk along the road,
when you lie down and when you get up.*

Deuteronomy 6:6-7

I love taking Ubers. With my passion to share my faith and talk
about Jesus, I enjoy having a captive audience. Probably 90% of
the time it turns into a Divine assignment as I allow the Holy Spirit
to direct conversation. Mostly I find Uber drivers enjoy conversation
and it's given me many wonderful testimonies. Sometimes they're
not Christ followers; sometimes they're atheists, sometimes wounded
Christians or fellow believers who need encouragement. But one thing
in common: they are all very surprised when I tell them that I rap.
And most are blessed when I'm able to share it with them. Remember,
Paul encourages the church in Ephesus to "make the most of every
opportunity" (Ephesians 5:16).

As I reflect on some scriptural precedent to share in this category
of sowing seeds, I couldn't find many of Uber ministry. LOL. But Jesus

often demonstrated sowing seeds of love, truth, and compassion on the road. In Luke's Gospel we have the story of blind Bartimaeus. Jesus is traveling along the road where a blind man is begging. He begins to call out to Jesus for mercy. Jesus' followers have little compassion and try to silence him. Yet Jesus demonstrates for us to stop for the one; to care for those who are in need. When asked by Jesus what he wants, the blind man exhibits faith to ask to be healed. To the astonishment of all, his sight is restored, and he follows Jesus down the road giving praise to God. (Luke 18:35-43) We carry God's presence so that wherever we go—on the road or about our everyday activities—we might sow seeds of truth and hope by the power of His Spirit.

Another passage takes place on the road to Emmaus where Jesus comes upon two disciples but is not recognized by them. They share what has just transpired with their beloved teacher who was crucified and yet rose from the dead. The stranger speaks truth into their hearts and minds, telling of prophets who foretold the suffering of Christ and God's purposes. Their eyes are opened as they break bread together, they recognize Jesus who then disappears from their sight. "Were not our hearts burning within us while He talked with us on the road and opened the scriptures to us?" (Luke 24:32)

One of the most familiar "on the road" stories Jesus shared to teach His listeners an important truth was the Parable of the Good Samaritan. Jesus is questioned by an expert in the Law as to the way to inherit eternal life. Jesus answers, "Love the Lord your God with all your heart and with all your soul and with all your strength and with all your mind; and love your neighbor as yourself" (Luke 10:27). He then asks Jesus, "Who is my neighbor?"

Jesus tells of a man traveling on the road to Jericho who is brutally attacked by robbers and left for dead. Along the road comes a priest who ignores the man and continues on his way. Then a Levite, who serves in temple worship, also comes traveling along that road but passes by as did the priest. But a Samaritan man—looked down upon by Jews—comes upon the injured man. He shows compassion and tends his wounds, places him on his donkey and brings him to an inn.

There he pays the innkeeper to take care of him and promises to pay for all expenses.

Jesus then asks, "Which of these three do you think was a neighbor to the man who fell into the hands of robbers?"

The expert in the law replied, "The one who had mercy on him."

Jesus told him, "Go and do likewise" (Luke 10:36-37).

I am grateful to use "on the road" experiences to share God's love with people, hear their stories, show compassion and encourage them as God directs. May we too, "Go and do likewise."

Sowing Seeds on the Road

The Lord himself goes before you and will be with you; he will never leave you nor forsake you. Do not be afraid; do not be discouraged. Deuteronomy 31:8

So, commit yourselves wholeheartedly to these words of mine ... Teach them to your children [and those you encounter daily]. Talk about them when you are at home and when you are on the road ... Deuteronomy 11:18-19 (words in brackets mine)

So, [Philip] started out, and on his way, he met an Ethiopian eunuch, an important official ...who had gone to Jerusalem to worship and on his way home was sitting in his chariot reading the Book of Isaiah the prophet. The Spirit told Philip, "Go to that chariot and stay near it." Then Philip ... heard the man reading Isaiah the prophet. "Do you understand what you are reading?" Philip asked . . . . So, he invited Philip to come up and sit with him. . . . Then Philip began with that very passage of Scripture [of a sheep led to the slaughter] and told him the good news about Jesus. As they traveled along the road, they came to some water. . . . Then both Philip and the eunuch went down into the water, and Philip baptized him. When they came up out of the water, the Spirit of the Lord suddenly took Philip away, and the eunuch did not see him again, but went on his way rejoicing. Acts 8:27-39 (selected verses)

On the Sabbath we went outside the city gate to the river, where we expected to find a place of prayer. We sat down and began to speak to the women who had gathered there. One of those listening was a woman from the city of Thyatira named Lydia, a dealer in purple cloth. She was a worshiper of God. The Lord opened her heart to respond to Paul's message. Acts 16:13-14

The Lord will keep you from all harm—he will watch over your life; the Lord will watch over your coming and going both now and forevermore. Psalm 121:7-8

Oops! Wrong Airport but Right Uber Driver – Washington DC (March 2012)

We were on the way to Kentucky where Alan was invited to speak at the Governor's Prayer Breakfast. Riding on the Metro to Reagan National Airport, Alan asked if I was sure I had the tickets. Yes, of course I do. But then something had me double check which airport we were flying out of as the Washington DC area has two. Oops! Bad mistake. We were flying out of Dulles International but were on our way to Reagan National. Ugh!

Quickly we got off the next stop and looked for a Taxi. No taxi as it was not a popular Metro stop. We decided to try Uber which was fairly new, and it took fifteen minutes for one to arrive. The driver heard our dilemma and said he would try his best to get us to Dulles, but would probably take forty-five minutes which would be cutting it very close to our boarding time. We had no choice and prayed we would make it. Conversation entailed and as we started sharing our faith, Hakim became excited and shared he was a believer in Jesus. What wonderful sharing followed as we all told testimonies of our great Lord and Savior. He was blessed to talk with us of spiritual matters and as we approached Dulles, we lifted up prayer for Hakim for God's blessing upon him and his loved ones. It was a meaningful time together during our Uber ride. And ... we made our plane which had been delayed thirty minutes. We arrived right when boarding was starting. Thank you, God, for providing Christian fellowship in unexpected ways. Thank you that providentially You had the plane delayed. Open our eyes to see how we might connect with those in the body of Christ wherever You have us.

❦

Uber Driver Great Fellowship – Houston, Texas (June 23, 2018)

After visiting my daughter in Houston, I put in a request for an Uber to bring me back to the airport. Alan was remaining an extra week with Jennifer and grandkids. Stephanie arrived and we got onto spiritual conversation pretty quickly. We shared our mutual love for Christ and talked about our faith journey for forty-five minutes. Her mother had been instrumental in imparting spiritual truth and passion into her life. I told her that I was passionate to share my faith with younger adults and that God surprised me with giving me two Gospel raps.

She was totally blown away with my "Jesus Rap"—she got tears and goosebumps from the Holy Spirit as I shared. I saw her wiping away tears as it moved her deeply, she said. I was blessed to be with this beautiful woman of God who desires to be a vessel of love to those God brings into her life through her Uber work. We also agreed how wonderful it was to be guided and directed by the Holy Spirit.

As we approached the airport Stephanie told me how after certain passengers leave her vehicle after the Uber ride, she will open the windows for spiritual cleansing of her vehicle. She made me smile and said, "After you get out Miss Sally, I'm not opening the windows. I want what you have to stay in." I told her my daily prayer is, "Holy Spirit possess me, use me, empty me and let my life reflect Jesus. God, be glorified in my life!" She got out of her car and hugged me, new sisters in Christ. I prayed for her—blessing and encouragement and greater fullness of the Holy Spirit.

Adib – Good Deeds versus God's Free Gift – Houston, Texas (January 7, 2019)

Another trip to Houston, another Uber driver. Adib was one of the talkative drivers and after casual chit-chat, we began discussing spiritual beliefs. He was of the Muslim faith, sincere in his beliefs and respectful of Jesus, whom he considered a great prophet. He shared about doing good deeds, but I said, yes, good deeds were important but righteousness is a free gift from Jesus as we choose to follow Him and trust in Him. Adib was very devoted, and it was hard to direct him toward Jesus as the only way to God. I felt led to say my "Jesus Rap" and he said, "Very nice, I've never heard anything like that before." Seeds were planted of Jesus God's Son and loving Savior.

❦

Christmas Trip After Alan's Homegoing – Massachusetts (December 2020)

After Christmas I flew to Massachusetts to visit my sister Irene and took an Uber from the airport to their home. I didn't mind as I assumed it would be a Divine assignment which it was. Kent, the driver, was a nice older man recently retired and was doing Uber part-time. We spent a few minutes of casual talk in which I shared that I had just lost my husband Alan on December 11th after an eight-year terminal illness. Quickly I brought the conversation to spiritual topics and shared my testimony with him—that I had been raised in a traditional church, but through a painful childhood, I had turned away from faith in God and had been a hippie in the 70s. This made him laugh. He shared that he doesn't go to church anymore but was raised Catholic.

Since he was open, I told him about my dear Alan who had served God faithfully for forty years and the privilege I had of partnering with this mighty man of God. I shared about the Holy Spirit giving Alan words of knowledge as when on the metro in DC Alan got the name "Daniel" and spoke life-giving words into a prodigal's life. Then in Desert Storm Alan heard God tell him to shine his flashlight ahead of his vehicle and he saw the prongs of a mine poking up from the sand. Lives were saved because Alan had a relationship with God and heard His voice.

Kent laughed when I told him that I rapped, and that God had given me this unique way to speak into the hearts of the younger generation. I asked if I could share it there in the car and he was quite intrigued to hear it. Well, he loved it and clapped—letting go of the steering wheel for a few seconds. Oh my!

At the end of the one-hour drive he said, "This was one of the most momentous rides I've ever had." How humbling to believe the life of Jesus is being seen. Thank you, Jesus. Please draw Kent and others like him who are searching back to yourself—use my life Lord to be a witness for you.

～⚹～

Uber Driver Teresa Enroute from Laporte – Iowa to Ohio (October 2022)

I was traveling from Chicago to my daughters in Toledo and had spent the night at a Holiday Inn. After breakfast, I went to the Uber app on my phone and requested a driver to take me an hour to a garden center on the way to Jennifer's. At first, no one picked up, so I walked around and waited. Then I tried again and Tara responded and came in twenty-five minutes. In the Uber we immediately got into conversation about faith and suffering: she almost died from an infection that led to sepsis. She was very close to death and was in the hospital for a month. She had been a nurse but was advised not to return to nursing as her lungs and heart had been affected. But I said, "Well, I'm going to pray for you before our trip ends that God would totally heal you."

We had wonderful fellowship sharing back and forth for the

remainder of the ride. She had been through two marriages that were difficult but had really grown in faith through all the trials in her life. She put her trust in the Lord and was grateful for His blessings. I could tell she had a beautiful heart to serve and care for others. I felt led to pray the "Blessing Prayers for Women" over her as we drove the last twenty minutes and then I prayed God's healing touch upon her and for God's will to be fulfilled over her life. She wiped away tears as I finished praying and said how grateful she was for the trip and for the time spent together. At the end I felt such love for and closeness to Tara. When we got to the garden store, she said she wanted to give me a hug. I said, "Yes, me too." We hugged, and I told her I loved her.

❧

Prayer

Thank You, Lord, that You present us opportunities to witness in ordinary day-to-day life and in our present culture where we can find ourselves on the road with strangers who drive Ubers. How meaningful life can be when we see with Your eyes people we encounter who need encouragement and are truly blessed by being with us because of Your abiding presence. You have reconciled us to our Father God through Your life and Your sacrificial death on the cross. Our ministry also is to sow the message of God's love and truth, praying our seeds would produce a harvest of souls brought into Your family. Thank You for the prayer You lifted up to the Father for Your followers: "I have made you known to them, and will continue to make you known in order that the love You have for me may be in them, and that I myself may be in them" (John 17:26). May the Holy Spirit embolden us "on the road" to sow seeds of compassion and love. Amen!

❧

11

God Still Speaks—
Can You Hear Him?

My sheep hear my voice, and I know them, and they follow me.

John 10:27 (ESV)

As followers of Christ, we have received the incredible gift of God's Holy Spirit. Being connected with the God of the universe in a profound and personal way grants us the privilege of living life on earth as Jesus did. By the Spirit Jesus received wisdom and knowledge from His Father enabling Him to fulfill God's purpose: bringing light, love, and truth to this broken world. God still speaks, and we also are able to hear God's voice and speak to our world. Recorded for us in the Gospel of John is an interaction between Jesus and Nathaniel, giving us an example of the supernatural gift of knowledge.

Jesus has just called Philip to come and follow Him (John 1:40). Philip in turn brings his friend Nathanael to Jesus. The dialogue is intriguing. When Jesus sees Nathanael coming, He says, "Here truly is an Israelite in whom there is no deceit."

This shocks Nathanael who asks, "How do you know me?"

Jesus answers, "I saw you while you were still under the fig tree before Philip called you."

Then Nathanael responds, "Rabbi, you are the Son of God; you are the king of Israel."   Jesus says, "You believe because I told you I saw you under the fig tree. You will see greater things than that."

Nathanael is so stunned with Jesus' revelation seeing him under the fig tree that he declares that Jesus is the Son of God and king of Israel.

A word of knowledge spoken over me years ago by a stranger declared that I was a modern-day Johnny Appleseed. This was a meaningful word of encouragement for me in my life and amused me in its significance. Johnny Appleseed was an itinerant evangelist traveling in the east in the first half of the nineteenth century, sowing literal apple seeds along with seeds of the Gospel of Jesus Christ. The person who shared this word with me was a stranger and did not know I grew up in Massachusetts in a small city only ten miles from Johnny Appleseed's birthplace. It blessed me to receive God's affirmation of this call on my life. I truly love spreading Gospel seeds wherever I go.

I have also received surprising words from strangers who saw me sharing my faith in Jesus in airports and grocery stores. Quite incredible because over the past decade, those are two of the places where Holy Spirit boldness comes on me and I joyfully witness to those God highlights to me.

The word of knowledge can be seen as the ability of one person to know what God is currently doing or intends to do in the life of another person. It can also be defined as knowing the secrets of another person's heart. Here is an explanation which shows the purpose of a word of knowledge: "God can use a word of knowledge in many different ways. It can be used to draw someone closer to God, increase faith, bring conviction, help in a difficult situation, open doors, and bring favor with a person or in a life situation."[5]

In this chapter you'll read two of my husband's powerful stories which are quite amazing. Alan had trained himself to hear God's voice clearly and often received words of knowledge for people. I believe these stories will bless you and increase the desire in your heart to be used with this supernatural gift that we might see people's lives transformed.

[5] Melissa Tumino, "The Powerful Gift of Word of Knowledge," Think About Such Things, accessed May 13, 2024, https:// thinkaboutsuchthings.com/gift-of-word-of-knowledge/.

Sowing Seeds as God Speaks

The Spirit gives life; the flesh counts for nothing. The words I have spoken to you—they are full of the Spirit and life. John 6:63

Now to each one the manifestation of the Spirit is given for the common good. To one there is given through the Spirit a message of wisdom, to another a message of knowledge by means of the same Spirit... 1 Corinthians 12:7-8

If anyone speaks, they should do so as one who speaks the very words of God. If anyone serves, they should do so with the strength God provides, so that in all things God may be praised through Jesus Christ. To him be the glory and the power for ever and ever. 1 Peter 4:11

So shall my word be that goes out from my mouth: It will not return to me empty, but will accomplish what I desire and achieve the purpose for which I sent it. Isaiah 55:11

The Lord said to me: "What they say is good. I will raise up for them a prophet like you from among their fellow Israelites, and I will put my words in his mouth. He will tell them everything I command him. I myself will call to account anyone who does not listen to my words that the prophet speaks in my name." Deuteronomy 18:7-19

Apply your heart to instruction and your ears to words of knowledge. Proverbs 23:12

Metro Train Rider Shocked by Words Spoken – Washington DC (2007)

An interesting God assignment happened in 2007 as my husband Alan was taking the subway home after work. He boarded the train, noticed a tough looking guy sitting at the end of the car and the name David popped into his mind. He said to himself, "No way, God."

He walked to the back, sat across the aisle from him, turned, and asked, "Is your name David?"

The man looked shocked and said, "Yeah, how do you know?" At that moment Alan realized God had given him this revelation for a reason and stepped out in faith boldly, sharing what the Holy Spirit revealed.

"David, God sent me here today to tell you that He loves you very much and has a destiny for you. But you're heading in the wrong direction, and you're doing things you shouldn't be doing. You've been running from God for a while. There's a church you're supposed to go to and if you don't go there this Sunday, you will never go to Heaven."

Suddenly tears started falling. "David, will you go? The Lord loves you and has a good plan for your life. David nodded his head as the tears continued falling, "Yes, yes." At the next stop Alan felt that he was to get off and leave David with that message from God. God still speaks!

಄಄

Seeing as God Sees – a Girl and a Piano – Portsmouth, Rhode Island (1996)

In 1996 my husband Alan was the guest preacher at a church in Portsmouth, Rhode Island. At the end of the service people were invited to come forward for prayer. A young woman came who Alan discerned was carrying a heavy burden and seemed tormented. He placed his hands on her face, closed his eyes and saw a vision of a living room with a piano and a young girl sitting at it playing. At the other end of the room was a young girl watching the pianist; she was wearing a frilly white dress and shiny black shoes. He told the woman what he was seeing, and she confirmed it was her family's living room. "Were you the pianist?" he asked. She said no, she was the observer.

The Holy Spirit then gave Alan knowledge that there was a spirit of resentment in her because her sister—who was an accomplished pianist—received her mother's affirmation. She was jealous and even admitted hating her sister. She confessed to daily inner turmoil since childhood. Because God had revealed this to my husband, Alan knew God wanted to set this woman free. He led her in confessing sins of resentment, jealousy and hatred against her sister. With no legal right now, the oppressive spirit left her and she was set free. God still speaks!

Word from God Surprises Store Employee – Toledo, Ohio (April 12, 2024)

While visiting my daughter in Ohio, God had a Divine assignment for us in a department store. We walked by a young male employee and asked him if he could direct us to a certain department, which he did. I felt led to share with him my "Prayers for Men" handout, asking if he might want to take it home and look at it later. He was hesitant, as he told us that he grew up in church but wasn't very religious now. I shared a little bit about the importance of faith and trusting in God and he said that he would take the handout and look at it later.

My daughter surprised me by telling Justin, "Hey, so sometimes God speaks to me and gives me a word for someone. Are you ok if I share it with you?" Justin said, "I guess so, sure." So Jennifer shared, "I saw two roads in front of you and a big decision up ahead. But I felt like God said, 'you will know which path to take, and it will be a blessing to you and your future.'"

Justin was shocked and literally jumped back and said, "That is so crazy—that's freaky. I just applied for a new job and I'm also thinking about being a cop. So, I'm applying to the police academy and waiting to hear back from them."

I followed up and shared that God had just made Himself known, making it obvious that He knew about Justin and these decisions for future work. Also, I told him that the Holy Spirit is so awesome— He gave my daughter those words to encourage him, concerning this decision to be made. The Holy Spirit is the Spirit of God dwelling in us and speaking through us, showing how He cared enough to speak through my daughter concerning Justin's future. God still speaks!

‏‎❧

McDonald's Divine Appointment – Gardner, Massachusetts (November 19, 2018)

I was sitting in McDonalds in my hometown in Massachusetts visiting my sister and waiting for my nephew to finish work. Without meaning to eavesdrop I heard snippets of conversation from a young woman in the next booth. "Drugs … who am I … identity."

The Holy Spirit led me to get up, walk up to her, and say, "Hi, excuse me, sometimes God points out people to me—could I talk with you? I'm a person of faith and love sharing with people about God's love." Well, with the boldness of the Spirit I asked if I could sit down. I shared that I lived in Kansas City but was visiting my hometown and had been a hippie in the 70's—into drugs, drinking, etc. But I discovered that I needed Jesus and it was possible to have a loving relationship with Him. So I humbly prayed to give my life to follow Him and He dramatically changed my life."

Then I said, "Would you believe I rap about God's love? Could I share my rap with you?" She and the man with her (she told me later it was her father) looked very surprised. I did my rap for her sitting in the booth as she stared at me. She really seemed to like it. I shared more about Jesus with her: "He is real. He loves you and wants to have an intimate relationship with you." (They seemed to have faith, but were somewhat hesitant.)

Marissa seemed moved by God. She smiled and told me, "Two days ago I prayed that God would give me a sign. Your coming over to talk and share your rap with me clearly was God's answer." (Oh God, thank you that I obeyed!) I encouraged her to seek Jesus and trust Him. Pretty amazing how God so clearly pointed her out to me and moved me to go up to her as His witness in McDonald's. Yay God!

Talking with my sister later, I realized that Divine synchronicity had come into play. Four years ago, I lived in my hometown for a year and met a woman named Denise in a store and became friends. I prayed with her several times for her family. This was Marissa's mother—my sister told me she remembered them from church. Marissa's parents ended up divorcing and left the church. But God had me be an answer to the prayer I had prayed four years ago with Denise, for her family to be touched by God. Holy Spirit, I am so grateful for how You empower and use us to be Your instrument of love and truth to the lost.

❧❧❧

Dana at Redemption Church – Perrysburg, Ohio (September 20, 2021)

At my daughter's church after morning service, I felt led to engage in conversation with a lovely woman sitting in front of me with her husband and son. I sensed during the service that she was burdened and felt God giving me a word of knowledge that she needed God's rest. After introducing myself, I shared that God wanted me to let her know how much He loved her. I also asked if I could share Deuteronomy 33:12 with her. "Let the beloved of the Lord rest secure in him for He shields him all day long. The one the Lord loves rests between his shoulders." She seemed surprised and a bit uncomfortable, but I hugged her, gave her a Scripture handout, and encouraged her to look up the Bible verse about seeking God's rest. I prayed a quick prayer and blessed her. Surprisingly the next day I got a very long email from her thanking me and telling me that the Lord had encouraged her. She appreciated that I shared with her even though it was outside of her comfort zone. God still speaks!

❧

Rest Stop the Holy Spirit Speaks – Asheville, North Carolina (May 28, 2024)

While driving in North Carolina looking for a rest stop, I asked the Holy Spirit for a word to share with someone I might encounter there. He gave me these words:

"I see you … I know you … I love you … I forgive you."

At the rest stop, I walked around to stretch my legs and I saw walking in front of me a middle-aged woman in dark clothes, long dreads, piercings. I engaged her in conversation – her name was Dionne and I told her God sometimes points out people and I felt he gave me a word to encourage her. I asked if I could share it with her.

"I see you … I know you … I love you … I forgive you."

She looked intently at me. I then told her about God's love and Jesus' life, relating my testimony and then felt led to share again the words God gave me. I gave her the Prayers for Women handout—she was quiet and seemed to be carrying a burden. She didn't say much, but I felt that she was the one to receive this message of God's love for the lost, the hope He offers and the true life found in Jesus Christ.

❧

Prayer

Holy Spirit, deepen my understanding and awareness of Your desire to speak today in and through my life. I want to be used to touch and even transform someone's life through words You give me to speak. Empower me in my life of faith and make me willing to take a risk as I yield to Your leadership. Thank You for the privilege of using my ordinary life to reveal You—my extraordinary God—in encouraging, strengthening, and helping others grow in faith. Jesus, give me words of knowledge that come from Your heart that others would come to know your love and goodness. Amen!

12

Blessed to Be a Blessing

Those who live to bless others will have blessings heaped upon them, and the one who pours out his life to pour out blessings will be saturated with favor.

Proverbs 11:25 (TPT)

There is an incredible promise God has given us in this verse from Proverbs 11:25—that blessings will be heaped upon you, and favor will saturate your life, if you live to bless others. That appeals to me, to you also? But too often people in our society live for themselves—desperately wanting to be blessed and experience the good life, but often finding that it evades them. We live at a time when words come forth that judge, criticize, and curse rather than bless. In government, media, sports, and entertainment this can be the norm. News segments that commend heroes and those who better society are usually tacked onto the last two minutes of an evening summary of the day's disheartening happenings. There is not much in our daily news to bless our spirits.

As a follower of Jesus Christ, my life has been so blessed even though I've had my share of trials and hardships. Blessed with experiencing the love of Father God possible through asking Jesus to be my Savior when I was twenty. Blessed with the wonderful gift of the Holy Spirit bringing radical change to my life: from darkness to light, depression to joy, despair to hope. Blessed with the most incredible husband who I was privileged to have for forty-six years before he went home to His Savior. Five years ago, out of gratitude for what God did for my life, I had the idea to bless people I encounter daily by handing out Scripture prayers: "Blessing Prayers for Women" and "Prayers to Bless and Honor Men." My previous chapters have made note of these handouts as they are one of the main ways I share my faith with strangers. To my delight, the reaction from people is so positive that I look forward to the almost daily opportunity to give these out in grocery stores, doctors' offices, parks, etc. Who doesn't want to be blessed, right? It has been a powerful resource to encourage hearts and minds, giving hope to those who may be downcast.

To bless is to speak God's will over someone's life and to ask for His gifts of health, protection, unconditional love, meaningful relationships, strength and grace for each day. The Biblical precedent of this was given to Jewish patriarch Abraham, who God called to become the father of nations. God declared to Abraham: "I will bless you and make your name great... and all people on Earth will be blessed through you" (Genesis 12:2-3). This passage foretells that all people on Earth will be blessed through the lineage of Abraham from whom would come Jesus the Messiah. The Israelites had it right because in their culture they knew the power of the spoken word of blessing. It was the Jewish custom that when the patriarch would approach their time to "be gathered to their fathers," (Judges 2:10) they would pronounce a blessing on their heir. What would that be like for you to receive your Father's blessing? Sylvia Gunter and Arthur Burk beautifully state this need we all have:

> The most profound blessing our spirit needs to receive and can receive is the Father-heart of God: His special creation of us, His kind intention toward us, His matchless love for us, His glory revealed in us... To know the Father-heart of God nurtures belonging, inclusion and worth.[6]

[6] Sylvia Gunter and Arthur Burk, *Blessing Your Spirit* (Birmingham: The Father's Business, 2005), viii.

Jesus demonstrated the spiritual significance of blessing in the Beatitudes, which were surprising and upside-down blessings He spoke to His followers as He began His ministry. He began with "Blessed are the poor in spirit for theirs is the Kingdom of Heaven" (Matthew 5:3) and continued with a total of nine blessings pronounced on His listeners. (You will find the full passage of the Beatitudes at the end of this chapter.) Throughout Jesus' ministry He revealed the power of the spoken word. Jesus took time to bless the children who were brought to Him: "And He took the children in His arms, put His hands on them and blessed them" (Mark 10:16). He blessed those who came to Him, demonstrating great faith; He commended them, granting their requests. After His resurrection as Jesus' ministry on Earth was at an end, Luke records, "He lifted up His hands and blessed them. While He was blessing them, He left them and was taken up into heaven" (Luke 24:50-51). Let's consider how-to walk-in Jesus' steps and live to bless others.

Sowing Seeds Through Blessing

If you pay attention to these laws and are careful to follow them, the Lord your God will keep His covenant of love with you … He will love you and bless you and increase your numbers. He will bless the fruit of your womb, the crops of your land—your grain, new wine and olive oil … You will be blessed more than any other people. Deuteronomy 7:12-14a

See, I am setting before you today a blessing and a curse— the blessing if you obey the commands of the Lord your God that I am giving you today; the curse if you disobey the commands of the Lord your God and turn from the way that I command you. Deuteronomy 11:26-28a

Blessed are you, Israel! Who is like you, a people saved by the Lord? He is your shield and helper and your glorious sword. Deuteronomy 33:29

May God be gracious to us and bless us and make His face shine on us— so that Your ways may be known on Earth, Your salvation among all nations. May the peoples praise You, God; may all the peoples praise You. May the nations be glad and sing for joy. Psalm 67:1-4a

Praise be to the God and Father of our Lord Jesus Christ, who has blessed us in the heavenly realms with every spiritual blessing in Christ. Ephesians 1:3

The Lord bless you and keep you; The Lord make His face shine upon you and be gracious to you; The Lord lift up His countenance upon you and give you peace. Numbers 6:24-26

T-Mobile Rep Links Prayer – Tornado Averted – Lee's Summit, Missouri (April 8, 2017)

Can our prayers impact people's lives beyond what we hope? I was shopping in a T-Mobile Store and engaged the rep in spiritual conversation after our transaction. No other customers were in the store, so before I left, I asked if I could pray for him. I prayed over him blessings of good health, God's love to touch him and his loved ones, for protection and well-being, for the Holy Spirit to give him strength. Well, I gave him one of my handouts with my email at the bottom. I rarely hear back from people but with Eric I did. I'm humbled by this email and was almost in tears when I read it. But how can it be that in fifteen years no one ever had prayed for this man? Jesus, teach us to pray for others so our lives will impact others for eternity.

Email from the T-Mobile Rep:

Hey this is Eric, I helped you with your phone the other day. I wanted to say thank you for the prayer the other day. I can't stop thinking about it!! Have worked in the retail industry for 15 yrs and never had someone pray for me. Monday night I was coming home from Wal-Mart with my son. I got home and realized that a pretty big storm was coming. So, I live in a house that is a slab with no basement, so I put my son back in the car and drive to my sister's house on 21st street. My son, two nieces, sister and brother-in-law went downstairs in the basement to take cover because the sirens were going off. Forty minutes of sitting downstairs we go outside to see what's going on and two blocks away the f3 tornado headed to our house changed directions. Who knows it could just be irony or perhaps your kind words saved my world. I live in Oak Grove, Missouri. Thanks again and God bless!! Hope you are enjoying your phone!

Waiting Area and Flight to Kansas City – Houston, Texas (June 23, 2018)

I sat next to Trent, a school principal, as I was waiting to board my flight home. He was a man of faith and we enjoyed sharing our faith journey. I asked if I could pray a blessing on his life, work and service to God. The lady next to me overheard and ended our prayer with an "Amen!" and smiled.

On the plane I sat with Kyle and had two hours of Jesus talk and faith. I spoke the "Jesus Rap," which surprised him. Then I shared the power of prayer and living the Spirit-filled life. While waiting for the bathroom, I spoke to the flight attendants Esther and Mark—both were Christians.

God gave me a word for Esther: "God is pleased with your servant heart. Even if those above you don't appreciate you, God is smiling down on you." She hugged me and thanked me. I asked if I could pray for her about anything. Yes! Her son Arthur had a bulging disc and was in great pain. I prayed for Arthur with Esther and she was grateful. Then I felt led to share the "Jesus Rap" with the flight attendants while standing by the restroom. They both loved it and thanked me. Such a blessing to be used to encourage them.

As I was leaving the plane, Esther thanked me and said how I had blessed her. Trent was behind me and he interjected, "She sat by me and blessed me too." Only Jesus in me deserves those kind words. I arrived home and cried for joy that in the Spirit that Jesus gives us, we have the privilege to be His ambassador wherever we go.

Target Employee Grieving Loss of Mom – Lee's Summit, Missouri (October 13, 2018)

Checking out with the young cashier, who asked how I was doing, and I said, "Great, I just came from a Bible study at a local church." She then told me that her dad was attending a Grief Share class at a local church. So, I asked who she had lost, and she said her mom. I told her how sorry I was and offered my condolences to her.

That opened up a conversation with this sweet young woman. I said my mom had died early in my life when I was seven years old from lupus. She was surprised and said that's what her mom died of, and she didn't know anyone else who had ever had that disease. We talked more. I said I'd written a book on suffering and that my dad turned to alcohol after mom died.

She said, "Oh my dad too. But he's doing better now. We attend a local house of prayer sometimes, and it is nice to be there and sit in a peaceful place of God's presence and listen to worship music."

I said it must be hard for her, and asked how she was managing. She said she was doing OK, growing to know God better and trusting that things will work out. I encouraged her that God doesn't waste the hard things that happen in our lives and is always with us.

I gave her my card, and said my book on suffering was on Amazon. Also I told her I rap and she said she would check it out on YouTube. Then I realized I could give her a book, so I told her I was going get her a copy from my car. I got it, gave it to her and she said she was seeing her dad that night and would share it with him also. She smiled and said, "You made my day." I am so blessed to be a blessing!

Christ the King Catholic Church – Topeka, Kansas (July 23, 2023)

Several times in the summer of 2023 God led me to attend Catholic Mass with my devout Catholic neighbor—I found it to be a new place for me to minister God's love and grace. I had a getaway in Topeka, Kansas where I was working on writing this book while my friend was away and her house was empty. The Holy Spirit put on my heart to attend mass at Christ the King Catholic Church only a few minutes away.

I was walking out after Mass and a man around my age was walking next to me using a walker. I heard him answer a friend, who had asked how he was, that it was terminal cancer. I turned to talk to him and asked if I could pray for him. I laid my hand on his shoulder and asked God to overcome the cancer, to touch his body according to the promises of the word, "They shall lay their hands on the sick and they shall recover." And I claimed Psalm 103, "Bless the Lord oh my soul, who forgives all our sins and heals all our diseases." I spoke healing power in Jesus' name over every organ, and over every system in his body, every cell in his body. He was very touched and shared how he had come back to faith recently because of the cancer and has been attending Catholic Church.

I shared that I had written a book on suffering and God's redemptive power to use it for good. I asked if he was a reader, he said, "Yes I love to read." He walked with me to my car and I gave him my book. We talked for a few more minutes about the purposes of suffering and he was very encouraged and blessed by the Lord. He asked if he could hug me and said, "You're such a blessing." I told him in the midst of grieving for my husband, I am blessed to share Jesus' love and care for others like Alan did—reaching out to bring Jesus' love to those around him. Lord Jesus, bless those who struggle with sickness that they might receive Your healing.

Prayer

Father God, use us as Your sons and daughters to be Your ambassadors on Earth. You have blessed us with salvation, redemption, and the Holy Spirit's empowerment that we might be a blessing to those around us. Empty us of self and worldly mindsets as we set our hearts on the harvest field before us. May we walk in Your footsteps during our years on Earth. Pour through us living water to those thirsting around us and show us how we can bring blessing to people You put in our path. Amen.

The Beatitudes from Matthew 5:3-12

Blessed are the poor in spirit, for theirs is the kingdom of heaven.

Blessed are those who mourn, for they will be comforted.

Blessed are the meek, for they will inherit the earth.

Blessed are those who hunger and thirst for righteousness, for they will be filled.

Blessed are the merciful, for they will be shown mercy.

Blessed are the pure in heart, for they will see God.

Blessed are the peacemakers, for they will be called children of God.

Blessed are those who are persecuted because of righteousness, for theirs is the kingdom of heaven.

Blessed are you when people insult you, persecute you and falsely say all kinds of evil against you because of me. Rejoice and be glad, because great is your reward in heaven, for in the same way they persecuted the prophets who were before you.

13

Final Thoughts:
How to Be a Seed Sower

*Now to Him who is able to do exceedingly abundantly
above all that we ask or think, according to the power that
works in us, to Him be glory in the church by Christ Jesus to
all generations, forever and ever.*

Ephesians 3:20-21

G od is awesome—He has entrusted us to be His ambassadors
throughout our life on earth. We have been given the
privilege to tell of God's great love and redemption, reconciling the
world to Himself in Christ, that we might have intimacy with God (2
Corinthians 5:18-21). My life turned around in 1974 when I received
His love, forgiveness, and grace. Out of gratitude I now live compelled
to know Christ more each day and to make Him known. This life
of faith and witnessing, which I've called sowing seeds, is not done
in our own strength but through the power of the Holy Spirit. Paul
expressed it beautifully in Ephesians 3:20—God's power is at work in
us and things beyond what we can imagine are possible by faith in our
all-powerful God.

I want to emphasize again—as I've done throughout my book—
the importance for each one of us in our daily lives to invite the Holy
Spirit to fill us, lead us, and use us each day. "You will receive power

when the Holy Spirit comes upon you, and you will be my witnesses" (Acts 1:8). Our life is not our own! It's too easy to forget that truth. Who and what are we living for each day? Joy is the gift we receive when we put Jesus first, others second, and yourself last. Joy is also a gift we can give.

As I am close to finishing the writing of this book, I just returned from a 6-week Holy Spirit-led adventure road trip for the purpose of being His witness on the road as I traveled to visit friends at eight locations on the East coast. God answered prayer and enabled me to sow many seeds—caring for the lost and hurting, bringing encouragement to the discouraged, and praying for many. God had led me to downsize, to put my remaining possessions in storage and go where He would lead me. Over and over God brought me joy as I walked as Jesus walked, attuned to the guidance of the Holy Spirit to stop for the "one" before me. Such deep fulfillment comes from being out in the harvest field.

My heart burns with desire to please God my Father, to share my love and devotion for Jesus Christ my Lord, and, for a season, to live sacrificially for the sake of the Gospel. My hope is that many of you dear readers, as you've read these testimonies, will receive activation by the Holy Spirit and empowerment in your faith-walk, so that you also may be bold to seek out those looking for life's true meaning. Remember this truth I shared earlier in my book: five-minute contact—lifelong impact. It is possible that God has a greater purpose for us! Our lives can make an impact for advancing God's Kingdom into our neighborhoods, communities, cities, and culture.

Are you willing to take a deeper step as a follower of Christ? Joy and fulfillment come with obedience. Even as a widow still grieving the loss of my dear husband Alan, my spirit has been lifted up by the kindness of God which surprises me with joy after Divine assignments. The same joy is yours as you keep in step with the Spirit, willing to boldly proclaim Christ, sowing seeds in your everyday life, and trusting God will reap a great harvest. The following I offer as practical ideas for your seed sowing.

CONVERSATION STARTER IDEAS: For those uncertain how to engage strangers in a waiting room, in a line, at the airport, or the grocery store, first begin by casually commenting or questioning on an everyday topic. For example, here's some that I might use:

"How's your day going?"

"What a beautiful day," or if it's not good weather, "Wow, what a storm we had last night."

"What a great game last night (during football, baseball season, etc.).

"Are you from the area?"

TRANSITION IDEAS TO SPIRITUAL TALK: Once you have started a conversation, try one of these openers.

"Hey, I'm a person of faith – where are you in your spiritual life?"

"Hey, I'm a person of prayer and I love to pray for people. Could I pray for you about anything in your life?"

"Hey, I'm a person of faith and I love to encourage people in their spiritual lives. I have these handouts with some amazing verses from the Bible. I'd love to give one to you if you're interested."

"I love to bless people—I try to follow Jesus and live as He lived. God loves people and invites people to receive new life through faith in Jesus Christ. He asks us to turn from sin, ask His forgiveness and walk in fellowship with Him as our Savior. He exchanges our sin for His free gift of righteousness."

It's as simple as that. Once you begin, the Holy Spirit will lead the conversation. Trust Him. It might feel uncomfortable at first, or maybe not, but once you allow the Holy Spirit to speak through you, it becomes addictive. You receive such a blessing yourself as you share life-giving words with others. May your faith be empowered to become a seed sower of excellence for God's glory. May the testimonies of this book encourage you—it's not about you having your Christian-walk perfected, but trusting God to use our weakness and brokenness through which He will be reflected. "Now He who supplies seed to the sower and bread for food will also supply and increase your store of seed and will enlarge the harvest of your righteousness." 2 Corinthians 9:10

Prayer

Father God, thank You for the testimonies I've just read in this book. Thank You for opening my understanding to a new way of seeing my God-ordained purpose on earth, which may include broken bumpers, mishaps, inconveniences, tears, and interruptions. With You, life can be an exciting adventure. Help me understand how those around me desperately need to hear the Good News—so many living without hope and with an emptiness in their soul. I want to be more obedient to speak of You in my everyday life as You lead. I believe it is possible as I welcome the Holy Spirit who equips me with power in my faith-walk, enabling me to love people as You love them, and see people as You see them. Take my mouth—may it speak truth; take my heart—may it feel Your compassion; take my daily agenda—let it allow for interruptions, which may be set up by You for the sake of sharing Jesus Christ. Let me through Your leadership become a seed sower, trusting You to water, nourish, and bring forth fruit and harvest from my life. I receive right now Heavenly impartation to empower my faith that I would be who You created me to be—a faithful witness of Jesus Christ. Amen!

Epilogue:
Miracle at the Senate

With gratitude for my husband Alan, who demonstrated so well the life of a seed sower, I want to close with this testimony from his faithful service (2003-2012) as Chief of Staff for the U.S. Senate Chaplain Barry C. Black.

The door opens and into the U.S. Senate chaplain's office walks Nkeeda, a Senate staffer on crutches. She is making her way with difficulty as her friend Stephanie follows behind carrying her belongings as well as Nkeeda's.

"Wow that looks challenging," says Dr. Alan Keiran, chief of staff for the Senate Chaplain. "What's going on?" he asks.

"Plantar fasciitis," she answers. "The doctor says I'll be on crutches for maybe six weeks."

"I don't think so. Come on over here I'm going to pray for you," Dr Keiran says.

Hobbling over to Dr. Keiran, Nkeeda sits, and he asks her to put her hands on her legs palms up. Placing his hands over hers, he starts to pray. Several minutes pass as Dr. Keiran prays for healing. He looks up asking, "Do you feel the warmth in your foot?"

Nkeeda, shocked that he's reading her mind, says, "Yes, I felt it from the beginning."

Dr. Keiran continues to pray, then asks once more how it feels. Instantly Nkeeda senses a warm sensation moving through her leg to her afflicted foot.

She wiggles her foot in her orthopedic boot and in disbelief declares, "I don't feel any pain!"

"Get up and walk," Everyone in the office is looking at Nkeeda as she stands a little wobbly, then walks across the office without crutches.

Her friend Stephanie shouts, "What in the…?!"

Nkeeda declares, "Wow, I can walk."

Stephanie looks like she's about to faint. Dr. Keiran asks for a percentage: "Is it twenty or thirty percent better?" She answers that it's at least sixty percent improved.

"Sit back down, we're going for one hundred percent." After more prayer and laying on of hands, God's miracle working power totally restores Nkeeda's foot. She takes off her boot and walks out of the office praising God.

Dr. Keiran lived out one of his favorite teachings: "The power of God is available to the people of God to achieve the purpose of God." Our God is still in the business of showing His power with life-transformation, supernatural healing, and hearts opened to new life that Christ brings us. Blessed to be a blessing! Are you ready for walking out the incredible privilege of being a seed sower in your life on earth? Go and live it!

About the Author

Sally Keiran is an author, teacher, and intercessor who worked alongside her husband, Navy Chaplain Alan N. Keiran, for twenty-three years in duty stations around the world. Her passion for prayer and unity in the Body of Christ led her to take organizational roles in the National Day of Prayer, March for Jesus, and Moms in Touch. She has been a conference and retreat speaker nationally and internationally. Sally is a loving mother, grandmother, and friend. An amateur bird watcher, Sally is always on the lookout for her flying friends while walking in nature or kayaking on a lake.

Her fervent passion is to see Christ's church emboldened by the Holy Spirit to actively share God's love and truth as the Gospel transforms our hurting world. She is the author of *Out of Suffering into Glory: God's Redemptive Purposes for Suffering*. Her Gospel rap can be viewed on Youtube at Sallys rap.

For Information and to download free resources, visit her on the Web at:

www.empoweredfaith.net

Contact Sally at:

Sally@empoweredfaith.net

www.ingramcontent.com/pod-product-compliance
Lightning Source LLC
LaVergne TN
LVHW041224080426
835508LV00011B/1071